Love Is No Accident

Wherever you are in life, whatever your situation, it is because you have chosen to be there. Whether you are alone and single, in a happy relationship or an unhappy one, you are there for one reason and one reason alone—you have chosen it. And, only you have the power to change it!

People make the mistake of thinking that they can only have love in their lives when they find it in someone else. They think that they will experience love as soon as the right person enters their lives. But the truth is, they will never find love in the people around them until they first find it within themselves.

BY ADAM J. JACKSON

The Ten Secrets of Abundant Happiness
The Ten Secrets of Abundant Wealth
The Ten Secrets of Abundant Love
The Ten Secrets of Abundant Health

Published by HarperPaperbacks

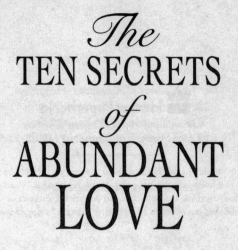

The TEN SECRETS *of* ABUNDANT LOVE

*A Modern Parable of Wisdom
and Happiness That Will
Change Your Life*

ADAM J. JACKSON

HarperPaperbacks
A Division of HarperCollins*Publishers*

🏭 HarperPaperbacks
A Division of HarperCollins*Publishers*
10 East 53rd Street, New York, N.Y. 10022-5299

HarperCollins®, 🏭®, and HarperPaperbacks™
are trademarks of HarperCollins*Publishers* Inc.

A trade paperback edition of this book was published in 1996 in Great Britain by Thorsons, an imprint of HarperCollins*Publishers*.

Cover and interior illustrations by Joan Perrin Falquet

First HarperPaperbacks printing: September 1996

Printed in the United States of America

Visit HarperPaperbacks on the World Wide Web at
http://www.harpercollins.com/paperbacks

❖ 10 9 8 7 6 5 4 3 2 1

For my wife, Karen,
and my children, Sophie and Samuel
with love always.

Contents

Acknowledgments

I would like to thank all those people who have helped me in my work and in the writing of this book. I am particularly grateful to:

My literary agent, Sara Menguc, and her assistant, Georgia Glover, for all their efforts and work on my behalf.

Everyone at Thorsons, but especially Erica Smith for her enthusiasm and constructive comments throughout the writing of the book, and Fiona Brown who edited the manuscript.

My mother, who always encouraged me to write, and remains a constant source of inspiration and love to me; my father for his encouragement, guidance and help in all my work, and all of my family and friends for their love.

And finally, to Karen—my wife, my best friend, and my most candid editor. Words cannot express my love for the one person who has always had faith in me and believed in my work.

A thought transfixed me: for the first time in my life I saw the truth as it is set into song by so many poets, proclaimed as the final wisdom by so many thinkers. The truth—that love is the ultimate and the highest goal to which man can aspire. Then I grasped the meaning of the greatest secret that human poetry and human thought and belief have to impart: *The salvation of man is through love and in love.*

Dr. Victor Frankl
Man's Search for Meaning

Introduction

The best and most beautiful things in the
world cannot be seen, nor touched ... but
are felt in the heart.

Helen Keller

We all crave love and loving relationships, perhaps
more than anything else, and we all search for that
one special relationship. Why is it, then, that so many
people live their lives in loneliness, searching, hoping,
but rarely finding? If love is what we desire most,
why are divorces and broken homes reaching unpar-
alleled numbers? Why are there so many single parents struggling to raise a family alone? Why is it that,
in cities filled with people, there are so many who feel
so alone, so isolated? Could it be that we have been
searching for love in the wrong place?

Contrary to popular belief, love is not the result of
fate or luck, and it is not something we fall into or out
of, it is something we create ... and we all have the
power to create it. We all have the power to love and
to be loved, we all have the ability to create loving
relationships. It doesn't matter where we find ourselves—single and alone or entangled in an unhappy,

stale relationship—life can change and we have the power to change it.

Unlike most other parables, many of the characters in this book are based upon real people although their names have of course been changed. It is my hope that their stories may inspire you, as they did me, and serve as a reminder that life can be all it was meant to be—filled with joy and wonder and love in abundance.

Adam Jackson
Hertfordshire
July 1995

The
TEN SECRETS
of
ABUNDANT
LOVE

The
WEDDING
GUEST

You probably wouldn't have noticed him; none of the other two hundred or so guests did. He sat alone at a table in the far corner of the room; a young man, in his late twenties, of average height, build and looks, dressed like most of the other men in the room in a black dinner suit.

Nevertheless, he felt conspicuous, sitting by himself. All of the other guests who had been sitting at his table during the meal were now up on the dance floor, but as the young man was shy by nature and didn't have a girlfriend with him, he decided to stay alone at the table and observe the party.

He couldn't deny that, by any standards, it had been a magnificent reception with no expense spared. Champagne cocktails followed by a six-course meal, with dancing in between each course to music played by a lively seven-piece jazz band. The venue itself was spectacular; the Royal banqueting suite of one of the most exclusive hotels in the centre of the city. Yet for all of its grandeur, the young man wasn't enjoying the occasion. He had never been a good mixer and being in a room with 200 strangers wasn't his idea of fun. The only person he knew in the room was the bridegroom who was an old friend he hadn't seen for years. In fact, he was surprised to have been invited at all.

He looked at his friend dancing cheek-to-cheek with his new bride. They looked so happy together and the young man couldn't help feeling envious, wondering when or if it would ever happen to him.

"Why is it," he thought to himself, "that other people marry, settle down and have children, but I can't sustain a relationship with a girl for more than a few months?" It wasn't as if he found it difficult finding girls to date, the problem was finding the right girl, a lasting relationship, someone with whom he would want to spend the rest of his life.

Sometimes, just thinking about his situation got him depressed. He imagined that there must be something wrong with him to be unable to have a lasting or meaningful relationship. Other times he told himself he was just unlucky. Perhaps, as friends had told him, it was all a matter of fate. Love was either written in his stars or it wasn't. There was nothing he could do to change it, either it would happen one day or it wouldn't.

There had only been one time, two years back, when he thought he had fallen in love with a girl, but even that affair only lasted three months. At the time he had been inconsolable, completely devastated, for weeks he had been unable to eat or sleep. And afterwards he had resolved never to allow someone to hurt him like that again.

As he sat watching all the couples in the room—some sitting with each other arm in arm, laughing; others dancing and singing—he told himself that he was better off being single and alone. After all, how many relationships really last? How many people stay together? At least being single, he wouldn't have to endure the pain of separation and loss. And he had his independence, he was free, he could go wherever and whenever he pleased.

But then, as he glanced around the room, the young man saw something that unsettled his thoughts, reminding him that love was possible, and that lasting, loving relationships did exist—in the middle of the dance floor, an elderly couple were holding each other tightly, and smiling into each other's eyes. As the young man watched them dancing, he wondered whether by some miracle there was somebody, somewhere waiting for him.

"You here by yourself?" The young man turned to find an elderly Chinese man standing next to him. He was a small man with pure white hair on the sides of his otherwise bald head and large smiling brown eyes that lit up his face when he smiled. Like most of the other men in the room he was wearing a black dinner suit, white shirt and black bow tie.

"Yes, I am," replied the young man returning the old man's smile.

"Me too," said the old man. "Do you mind if I join you?"

"Be my guest," answered the young man.

"Lovely wedding isn't it?"

"If you like that sort of thing," said the young man.

"Why would you not like a wedding celebration?" asked the old man.

"Well, it's all a bit of a farce these days isn't it?" the young man said, leaning back in his chair.

"What is?" asked the old Chinese man.

"Marriage."

"A marriage is only a farce if the couple don't love each other," said the old man.

"Love!" exclaimed the young man. "What is love? People fall in and out of love all the time. One day they're devoted to each other, and the next day they can't stand the sight of each other. If you ask me," said the young man, "love is overrated, all it seems to cause is heartache and misery."

"It is easy to be cynical," replied the old man, "but I promise you that there is no greater mistake you can make in this life than to be cynical about love." The young man turned to face the old man. "And why is that?" he asked.

"Take it from me," said the old man, "when you reach the end of your life, the only thing that will have any significance will be the love you have given and received. In your journey into the next world, the only thing you will take with you is love and the only thing of value that you will leave behind in this world is love. There is nothing else. I have known people happily endure many hardships in their lifetime, but I have yet to meet a person who can endure a loveless life.

"This is why love is the greatest gift in life," explained the old man. "It gives meaning to your life. It's what makes life worth living."

"I'm not so sure," mumbled the young man turning away.

"Why not?" asked the old man.

The young man remained silent for a moment before answering. "You know what I think; I think falling in love is a romantic myth. We're all led to believe that one day we'll meet someone and fall in love, but it rarely happens. And when it does happen, it doesn't last."

"Ah . . . I see," said the old man. "Of course, you're absolutely right. Falling in love is a romantic myth!"

The young man turned to face the old man. "Hold on a minute," he said. "I thought . . . "

"Love is not something we fall into," continued the old man, smiling. "It is something we create, and we all have the ability to create it. People make the mistake of thinking that they may 'fall in love'; they imagine that one day they will walk down the street and see someone and pow! But that's not love."

"What is it then?" interrupted the young man.

"Physical attraction, infatuation. Definitely not love! Of course, love can grow out of a mutual physical attraction, but real love can never only be physical. To love—to really love—you need to understand a person, you need to know them and respect them. You need to be genuinely concerned for their welfare. It's like apple pie."

"What do you mean?" asked the young man.

"Well, do you think you can tell how good an apple pie is just by looking at it?" replied the old man.

"Well, no. I'd want to taste it as well," said the young man.

"Of course. In other words you need to know what it is like on the inside as well as the outside, you agree?"

"Yes."

"And the same is true of people," explained the old man. "You can't tell what they're like by their outward appearance alone. To love someone completely you need to see them on the inside—their nature, spirit or soul. These are things that cannot be seen with the eyes. In Love, the essential things can only be seen with your heart.

"This is why lasting, loving relationships are not coincidental, they don't just happen, and they are not the result of luck. They are nurtured and built."

"How?" demanded the young man.

"When I was a boy, my mother taught me the golden rule of love," explained the old man. "'It was very simple,' she used to say. 'If you want to be loved, you must be loving.'"

"We all have the power to love and be loved and to create loving relationships in our lives. That is why it is so sad when people choose to live without it."

"How can you say that?" argued the young man turning back to face the old man. "Why would someone choose to live without love?"

The old man looked directly into the young man's eyes and answered: "Some people choose not to love rather than risk the pain that comes with separation and loss." The young man felt his face flush and his throat tighten at the old man's words. He felt uncomfortable, it was almost as if his mind was being read.

"I assure you," said the old man. "that love is readily available to everyone, but it is something we must choose." The old man nodded toward a couple on a nearby table who were having a heated argument. "There you see a good example; two people who prefer to win an argument than to win love. Life is full of choices. We can choose to be right or we can choose to be loved, we can choose to forgive or we can choose to avenge, we can choose to be alone or we can choose company. It's all about choices. People who do not have loving relationships in their lives very often, consciously or subconsciously, choose their situations."

"People choose their situations?" repeated the young man.

"Of course. Wherever you are in life, whatever your situation, it is because you have chosen to be there. Whether you are alone and single, in a happy relationship or an unhappy one, you are there for one reason and one reason alone—you have chosen it. And only you have the power to change it!

"Many people make the mistake of thinking that they can only have love in their lives when they find it in someone else. They think that they will experience love as soon as the right person enters their lives. But the truth is, they will never find love in the people around them until they first find it within themselves.

"What you are is what you get in life, and what you get is what you are. Relationships don't bring love to us, we bring love to relationships. When we become loving, loving relationships inevitably follow. This is why anybody can love and be loved, and anybody—whatever their circumstances in life—can create loving relationships."

"That may be so," said the young man, "but you still have to be lucky enough to meet the right person, don't you. You know, someone who you find attractive."

"Luck doesn't enter into the equation," said the old man.

"Okay, fate then."

The old man smiled. "Fate can lend a helping hand, and it usually does, but you must play your part too. You are not going to meet anyone sitting alone in the corner of the room, you must get up and make it happen."

"That's not always so easy," protested the young man.

"Nobody said it was easy," answered the old man. "But if you want love, you have to let go of your fears, and seize the opportunities in life."

"What opportunities?" asked the young man.

"In my country, there is an old story of a man who was visited one night by an angel who told him that great things lay ahead in his life: he would be given opportunities to receive great riches, to earn a prominent and respected position in society, and to marry a beautiful wife.

"All his life the man waited for the promised miracles, but nothing happened, and he eventually died a lonely, impoverished old man. When he reached the gates of heaven, he saw the angel who had visited him all those years before and protested to him. 'You promised me great riches, a high social position and a beautiful wife. All my life I waited . . . but nothing happened.'

"'I gave no such promise,' replied the angel. 'I promised you *opportunities* for riches, a respected position in society and a beautiful wife, but you let them pass you by.'

"The man was mystified. 'I do not know what you mean,' he said.

"'Do you remember you once had an idea for a

business venture but you feared failure and did not act upon it?' said the angel.

"The man nodded. 'Because you refused to act upon it, the idea was given several years later to another man who did not allow fear to stop him, and you will recall that he became one of the richest men in the kingdom.'

"'And, you may recall,' said the angel, 'a time when a great earthquake hit the city, destroying the great buildings and leaving thousands of people trapped. You had the opportunity to help find and save other survivors, but you feared that in your absence looters would raid your home and rob you of all your possessions, and so you ignored pleas for help and stayed in your home.'

"The man nodded, reminded of his shame. 'That was your great opportunity to save hundreds of people's lives which would have led to you being honored by all of the survivors in the city,' said the angel.

"'And, do you remember a woman, a beautiful red-haired woman to whom you were intensely attracted. She, who was like no other you had ever seen before or afterwards, but who you thought would never agree to marry the likes of you and so, in fear of rejection, you passed her by?'

"The man nodded again, but now tears were in his eyes. 'Yes, my friend,' said the angel, 'she would have been your wife and through her you would have been blessed with many beautiful children and with her you would have multiplied the happiness in your life.'

"We are all surrounded with opportunities every

day—including opportunities for love—but often, like the man in the story, we allow fear to stop us taking them."

"Fear?" repeated the young man quizzically.

"Yes. Fear. We don't reach out to people for fear of rejection, we don't communicate our feelings for fear of ridicule, and we don't commit ourselves to another for fear of the pain of loss."

The young man couldn't help thinking about all those occasions when his fear of being rejected had stopped him from talking to girls to whom he had been attracted. He exhaled sharply, upset about all of the missed opportunities.

"But," continued the old man, "we have one advantage over the man in the story."

"What's that?" muttered the young man.

"We are still alive. We can begin to take those opportunities. We can begin to create our own opportunities."

The young man could certainly relate to a lot of what the old Chinese man had said. He had always thought that love and loving relationships were all a matter of luck or fate. You either met the right person or you didn't. You see someone, are instantly attracted to them and fall in love; that's how he thought it worked, but now, after listening to the old man, he wasn't so sure.

The old Chinese man stood up. "You cannot have a loving relationship unless you first learn to love. Once you become loving, the relationships will inevitably follow."

"And you say anyone can learn to love," said the young man.

"Of course," smiled the old man. "It is the most natural state in the world to love—to love yourself, to love others and to love life. Whatever our circumstances, whatever our position in life, we all have the power to love and be loved, and to enjoy love in abundance. All we need to know are the secrets."

"What secrets?"

"The secrets of Abundant Love."

"Secrets of Abundant Love?" said the young man. "What are they?"

"The secrets of Abundant Love were first spoken of by ancient sages and prophets thousands of years ago. They are ten principles through which you can create not just love in your life, but love in such abundance that it will be with you throughout your life."

"You're joking aren't you?" said the young man.

"You're saying that anyone can find love and loving relationships?"

"No. I am saying that anyone can *create* love and loving relationships," replied the old man.

"But how can you be so sure?" asked the young man.

"If I clap my hands will they not make a sound? If I push this table, will it not move? There are laws in Nature, Universal laws which govern everything from the motion of the waves to the setting of the sun, everything is governed by precise unerring laws. Scientists have discovered many of these laws—laws of physics, laws of motion, laws of gravity. But there are other laws too—laws relating to human nature, to health, to happiness and . . . there are also laws relating to love."

"Laws relating to love?" exclaimed the young man.

"If these 'laws', as you say, exist, why don't we all know about them?" asked the young man.

"Because sometimes we lose our way in life. Sometimes we become disheartened and disillusioned, and we forget and need to be reminded.

"Without love in your life," said the old man, "the world can be a very cold and lonely place. But with love, the world becomes a paradise. Thornton Wilder, one of the great American playwright once wrote: 'There is a land of the living and a land of the dead, and the bridge is love . . . the only survival, the only meaning.' Follow the secrets of Abundant Love and you will find that meaning and transform your world and your life."

"How?" asked the young man.

The old man smiled as he handed the young man a piece of paper. The young man looked at it carefully, but all it contained was a list of ten names and telephone numbers. He turned it over, expecting something more, but the other side was blank.

"What's this?" he said, looking up again, but . . . the old man was no longer there. The young man stood up and surveyed the room, he even stood on his chair to get a better look, but the old man wasn't to be seen. He waited at the table, half expecting the old man to return, but after thirty minutes had passed, he knew he wasn't going to see the old Chinese man again that evening.

Before he left, the young man said goodbye to the bride and bridegroom. After thanking them for inviting him and giving them his best wishes, he asked if either of them knew an old Chinese man. Both of them were certain that there hadn't been an old

Chinese man on their invitation list. The young man deduced that the old Chinese man must have been a waiter, so on his way out, he asked the head waiter where he could find the elderly Chinese man on his staff. But he also had never heard of such a man and certainly didn't have anyone by that description working for him.

The young man was intrigued. Who was the old Chinese man? Where was he from? And what were the secrets of Abundant Love of which he had spoken? As he left the wedding celebration, clutching a piece of paper with ten names and ten phone numbers, he knew there was only one way he would be able to find out.

The
POWER
of
THOUGHT

The following day the young man telephoned all of the people on the list. He was nervous and more than a little embarrassed calling ten total strangers and asking them about "secrets of Abundant Love", but to his utter amazement, they all seemed to know exactly what he was talking about and appeared to be genuinely delighted that he had called them. He arranged to meet each of them in turn over the following weeks.

The young man was particularly curious to meet the first person on his list. Dr. Hugo Puchia was a retired professor of sociology, well known in the academic community for his outspoken views on human relations. He had written several best-selling books on the subject and was often invited to appear on radio and TV talk shows. The essence of Dr. Puchia's argument was that humanity, in its quest for scientific and economic progress, had all but ignored the essential things in life. He often quoted the ancient Cree Indian prophecy:

Only after the last tree has been cut down. Only after the last river has been poisoned. Only after the last fish has been caught. Only then will you find that money cannot be eaten.

Dr. Puchia was a large gregarious man in his mid-sixties. He had shoulder-length, flowing white hair and a gentle, almost boyish face which took twenty years off his age. He greeted the young man with open arms, hugging him as if he was a long-lost friend. The young man was unsure how to react. He was not used to hugging total strangers; in fact, he was not used to hugging anybody, even his own family. Greetings were usually confined to rather stoic handshakes.

"So you met the old man yesterday?" said Dr. Puchia, inviting the young man to take a seat. "How was he?" he asked.

"Absolutely fine, as far as I could tell," answered the young man as he sat down. "Who is he? Where does he come from?"

"Your guess is as good as mine. I only met him once and that was over thirty years ago. But he changed my whole approach to teaching and to living.

"I met him shortly after I began teaching here at the university. I had been assigned to look after six classes of first year students. Ten weeks into the term, I noticed that one of the students was missing. She was a pretty, vivacious and intelligent young girl whose work revealed great sensitivity. It was the third week running that she hadn't turned up for class; I asked the students who sat next to her if they knew where she was and would you believe that not only did they not know, none of them seemed even to care. They didn't even know her name!

"After class that day I went to the administrator to try and find out where the student was and why she had not come to class. 'I'm so sorry, I thought you knew,' the administrator said, taking me aside. She took me into her office and told me that my student had committed suicide two weeks earlier. That beautiful young girl had thrown herself off of the top of a ten-story apartment building.

"I sat down in the lobby, shocked by the news, wondering what could possibly make a student with so much potential end her own life. I don't know how long I had been sitting there before I noticed him sitting next to me."

"Who?" interrupted the young man.

"The old Chinese man," said Dr. Puchia. "He asked me what was bothering me and so I told him the story. He sat there in silence for a few moments, and then he turned to me and said something I shall never forget. 'You know,' he said, 'we teach students how to read and write, and add and subtract, we teach them what we think are the essentials of a good education, but we neglect the most important thing of all . . . how to love.'

"His words hit me like a sledgehammer. It was something I intuitively had felt but hadn't been able to articulate. We talked about love and life for some time and it was through the old man that I first heard about the secrets of Abundant Love—ten timeless principles through which we can bring love into our lives and into the lives of those around us."

"You mean to say these 'secrets' really do work?" interrupted the young man.

"Well, they did for me and I have hundreds of students who can testify to how these secrets helped them as well," explained Dr. Puchia.

"It sounds unbelievable; too good to be true," said the young man. "I mean, if it is that easy, why doesn't everyone follow them?"

"That's a good question," answered Dr Puchia. "Deep down in our soul, we all want love more than anything else in life, but sometimes I guess we just forget. We get side-tracked in pursuit of other goals— like our careers, or more money and the accumulation of wealth. We pursue leisure and entertainment and lose sight of the more important things in life, and what could be more important than love?"

The young man wrote down some notes as Dr. Puchia continued.

"Before the old Chinese man left, he handed me a piece of paper containing a list of names and phone numbers. I contacted all of the people on the list in turn over the following weeks and through them I learned simple, practical ways of experiencing love in abundance. Ways through which we can learn to build lasting, loving relationships. All of the ten secrets of Abundant Love are equally important, but the one which had the greatest impact on my life was . . . the power of thought."

"Thought?" repeated the young man.

"Yes. It is a simple, but undeniable fact that we

become what we think about. If you have angry thoughts, you will experience anger, if you have exciting thoughts, you will experience excitement, if you have happy thoughts, you will experience happiness . . . and if you have loving thoughts, you will experience love. Change your thoughts and you change your experiences. It's that simple."

The young man raised an eyebrow. "That's easy enough to say, but I'm not so sure it is easy in practice."

"You are right, it isn't always easy, which is why it is written that 'He who conquers his own spirit is greater than he who conquers cities.' But it can be done. We all choose our thoughts, but sometimes while growing up we are taught to choose the wrong thoughts. We are taught to judge other people, to discriminate against people who are different. But children don't care for differences in creed or color, they just see people. Love a child and the child will love you back because it is part of our nature to love one another. The problem is that a child's perception of love is determined primarily by their parents."

"How do you mean?" asked the young man.

"Well, the way in which parents treat each other and their children forms the basis of a child's perceptions of love. If children are continuously shouted at or slapped, they will invariably believed that it is acceptable, loving behavior to shout at or slap someone else. And that is why we often have to re-learn what love really is and what it means to be loving. We have to change our beliefs and attitudes towards love."

"But how can you undo years of conditioning?" asked the young man.

"The place to start to change your attitudes and beliefs and thus your thoughts is by affirmations."

"What is an affirmation?"

"An affirmation is a statement that you affirm aloud or to yourself which, if repeated often enough, will change your thoughts and beliefs. For instance, if you believe that you can't form lasting, loving relationships, you can begin to change that by affirming:

'I create love in my life by being loving. Today I will be loving toward everyone I meet.'

'Loving relationships come easily to me.'

or 'I have the power to create loving relationships in my life.'

"And if you don't believe that you will ever find your ideal partner or soul-mate, you could affirm, 'My ideal partner will enter my life at the right time and in the right place.'

"Affirmations change our thoughts and subconscious beliefs, our thoughts determine our actions, our actions produce our behavior and our behavior forms our destiny."

"How often do you need to repeat an affirmation for it to start working?" asked the young man, intrigued by this technique.

"As often as possible. Some people even write them down and put them in certain places in their cars or on the refrigerator door so that they will always see and read them. The minimum, though, is three times a day—once in the morning upon waking, once during the day and once again last thing at night."

"So all you need to do to change your thoughts is repeat affirmations?" said the young man.

"No. Affirmations help change your subconscious

beliefs, but you must also consciously consider what love means to you and what it means to love someone. It seems a little obvious, but in my experience, very few people give it much thought. What, for example, would be your answer?"

The young man hesitated. "Erm ... well ... let me see ... to love someone is to care for them, to be there when they need you, to help them."

"Excellent," said Dr. Puchia. "In other words, to act towards their highest good. But can you do that—can you care for someone, or help them—if you don't first think about what their needs are?"

"No. I suppose not."

"Therefore, if we want to love anyone or anything, the first and most crucial thing we must do is to think about them and consider their needs and desires.

"When I began my career," continued Dr. Puchia, "in my naivete I thought that teachers were supposed to teach subjects—be it mathematics, physics, geography or sociology—but I soon learned that a good teacher doesn't teach subjects, he or she teaches students. Each student has his or her own individual needs, they have different levels and ways of understanding, and a good teacher takes these into account otherwise the students will become bored or frustrated.

"The same is true in life; if we want to have loving relationships, we need to consider the needs of other people. And to do that, we need to put ourselves in their shoes, we need to try and look at things from their point of view. For example; a lot of people feel trapped in an unloving relationship and complain that their partner doesn't love them, but if they were to ask themselves, 'what can I do for my partner?'

rather than 'why doesn't he/she do such and such for me?' invariably they would find that their partner would feel loved and become more loving towards them. The problem is that most of the time we think of our own needs and not other people's. If we don't think about other people's needs it's difficult to be loving toward them.

"You see," continued Dr. Puchia, "everything begins with a thought—loving thoughts lead to loving actions and loving experiences."

"Yes, but there is one problem," said the young man. "Your thoughts can't help you find or create a loving relationship."

"You would be surprised," answered Dr. Puchia. "Quite the contrary, your thoughts will not only help you attract loving relationships, they will also help you recognize the woman of your dreams when she comes into your life."

"I don't understand," said the young man.

"Well, everyone hopes to find that one special love that will last forever, you agree?"

The young man nodded.

"So, who is your one special love?"

"I don't know. That's my problem," said the young man. "I don't have one."

"You do," answered Dr. Puchia, "I assure you. It is just that you haven't met her yet. The problem is, when that girl does walk into your life, how will you recognize her?"

"How does anybody know whether a person that they meet will be the one for them?" replied the young man.

"The only sure way that I know of," said Dr.

Puchia, "is to know who your ideal person is before you meet them. And the only way to do that is to have thought about the qualities you require in a person."

"What sort of qualities?" said the young man.

"Physical, mental, emotional and spiritual qualities. For example; would she be dark or fair? Large or small? What color eyes would she have? Or perhaps her physical qualities don't matter so much to you. But what sort of job or hobbies and interests would she have? Would she need to have certain spiritual beliefs? And what about her temperament, would she be extroverted or introverted? Would she need to be intelligent?"

"I have never really given it much thought," admitted the young man. "Is it really that important?"

"Absolutely," assured Dr. Puchia. "If you don't know what sort of person you want to spend your life with, how are you going to recognize her when she comes along?"

"But don't you just know when you meet someone whether they are the right person?" argued the young man.

"Perhaps some people do," said Dr. Puchia, "but even they will have created some sort of mental image of their ideal partner beforehand. Without giving thought to the qualities of your ideal partner, you can be easily swayed by sexual attraction, infatuation or simply by the fear of loneliness, and as a result end up with the wrong person.

"For example, it might be important to you that your partner should love animals. Then you meet someone who you are immediately attracted to, but you soon find out that they hate animals. You would know that, regardless of how sexually attracted you were to them, they are not your ideal partner.

"You see love is not blind, but lust and sexual attraction are; if you hadn't thought about the things that you require in a partner, you could easily end up with someone completely incompatible. On the other hand, if you build up a mental picture of the person with whom you would like to share your life, you are more likely to know them when you meet them."

"But isn't it a bit limiting to have an image of an imaginary partner?" said the young man. "I mean, how likely is it that you will meet your ideal partner?"

Dr. Puchia smiled. "It is not likely at all . . . it is certain! This is the essence of the power of thought—to attract something or somebody into your life, you must first imagine that they are already yours. Of course, some of the qualities on your list of an ideal partner may not be very important to you, but at least creating a mental picture of your ideal partner allows you to consider what qualities *are* important to you.

"It's like shopping in a supermarket. If you don't know what you want, or the things that are important for you to get, you can easily be influenced by the advertising and promotions, and probably buy all sorts of things you don't even need. You might come home without any of the essential items. Whereas, if you know what you want beforehand, you'll go straight to the relevant section and get it. The same happens in relationships; if we go through life without thinking about the qualities we want from a person, we may be influenced by physical or sexual attraction and only later, when the attraction has faded, discover that the partner we have chosen doesn't have any of the qualities that are important to us. But if we have thought about the qualities we want from a partner, we are more likely to recognize the right person when we meet them."

The young man wrote down some notes as Dr. Puchia continued. "Love in your life and in your relationships shouldn't be a struggle; true, it needs to be worked at—if we want love we have to do the things necessary to create love—and that I suppose is what the secrets of Abundant Love are all about; they remind us of the essential things we need to work at that will create love."

"And choosing the right thoughts is one of them?"

"That's right! Your ability to love and be loved, to create lasting, loving relationships, or to attract your ideal partner all begin with the power of your thought."

Later that evening the young man summarized the notes he had taken of his meeting with Dr. Puchia.

The first secret of Abundant Love—the power of thought.

Love begins with our thoughts.

We become what we think about. Loving thoughts create loving experiences and loving relationships.

Affirmations can change our beliefs and thoughts about ourselves and others.

If we want to love someone, we need to consider their needs and desires.

Thinking about your ideal partner will help you recognize her when you meet her.

• • •

His mind began to wander as he imagined what his ideal partner would be like—her looks, her personality, her likes and dislikes, her beliefs. As he closed his eyes, an image came into focus; she was beautiful, a little shorter than himself, with shoulder length auburn hair, large green eyes with a captivating smile. She was confident, kind and generous. She was intelligent, although not too serious, affectionate and compassionate. She loved animals, was concerned about the environment and liked the simple pleasures in life like walking in the countryside and sitting in on a cold winter's night next to an open fire.

The young man wrote these characteristics down on a piece of paper and sat back and re-read them. "Hmm," he murmured to himself, "if only . . . " and he folded the paper and placed it neatly on his bookcase.

The
POWER
of
RESPECT

The second name on the young man's list was a woman by the name of Dr. Millie Hopkins. Dr. Hopkins was a professor of psychology at the city university, the first woman to be appointed to the position of professor in the history of the university. She was an extremely popular professor, well loved and respected by students and staff alike. It was obvious from the intonation of her voice that she was delighted to receive the phone call from the young man and she insisted on setting aside some time the following day to meet him. They agreed on 5 pm at Dr. Hopkins' office on the university campus.

Despite her 64 years of age, Dr. Hopkins seemed to have the energy and enthusiasm of a first-year under-graduate. Her voice became animated and excited at the first mention of the old Chinese man. She was a small, broad, well-built woman, smartly dressed in a classical navy suit and white blouse. She had shoulder-length auburn hair tied back and, although heavily lined, she had a warm, friendly face.

"I met the old Chinese man nearly 20 years ago," she told the young man. "I was a quite different person then; I was a drug addict living on the streets."

The young man's jaw dropped in utter astonishment. "You are joking aren't you?" he asked nervously.

"Not at all," she replied without a hint of shame or embarrassment. "I lost count of how many times I was in and out of hospitals from drug overdoses and each time I went straight back out on the street and did it again.

"Then one day I woke up in a hospital bed after having my stomach pumped yet again, and there was a doctor sitting by my side, holding my hand. He had a kind, gentle face and spoke softly with genuine concern. He was the first person who had shown any real interest in me as a person. It was the first time for so many years that somebody had talked to me, face to face, as a human being. And that is why I will never forget the old Chinese man.

"We talked for a long while; I told him things I hadn't told anyone before—about my family, my childhood, my life on the streets. Everything. And do you know just talking about it all to him made me feel better. He said he had some friends who would be able to help me. He gave me their names and telephone numbers and so I contacted them. And thank God I did, because they showed me how to live again."

"You mean the secrets of Abundant Love?" asked the young man.

"Yes. I learned that the main reason why there was no love in my life was that I didn't love myself. That is why the second secret of Abundant Love was so important to me . . . the power of respect.

"You see I had no respect for anyone or anything. And if you have no respect, you have no love. You cannot love anyone or anything unless you first respect them. And the first person you need to respect is yourself. If you don't respect yourself, you cannot love yourself; and if you don't love yourself, it is very difficult to love other people."

The young man made notes as Millie continued. "And that was my biggest problem—I didn't love or respect myself."

"Why not?"

"I think it all went back to my childhood," explained Millie. "I was an illegitimate child and my mother remarried when I was three years old. She had always been ashamed of me, and my stepfather, for some reason I shall never know, positively hated me. I remember when I was six years old, my mother was cuddling my stepsisters and I ran over to be included. Suddenly I felt a violent shove on my back and I fell on the floor. I shall never forget the face of my stepfather towering over me as he said 'She's the mother of my children now, you ugly bastard.'"

"What did your mother say?" asked the young man, who could hardly believe what he was hearing.

"Absolutely nothing! She ignored me and kept on cuddling my stepsisters as if I wasn't there. It's hard to believe, isn't it, that parents can be so cruel, but I promise you that I know of people who have suffered far worse things from their parents. I can't say I was regularly beaten, but I was given no love or affection. To all intents and purposes I was neglected and rejected by my own family.

I felt rejected, unloved, and so I hated life. It's a common problem, you know. Many people don't respect themselves. They either don't like their appearance or their voice or personality or intellect and so they lose self-respect and consider themselves to be inferior to others. That is why I had to learn to respect myself and love myself before I could experience love from anyone else."

"But how did you learn to respect yourself?" asked the young man. "I can't imagine that it's an easy thing to do."

Millie smiled, "You're right. It is not always easy, but it can be done. We have to learn to accept ourselves, appreciate ourselves regardless of what other people might say about us. We have to learn that everyone and everything has a place on this earth. We are all unique. Did you know, for instance, that there has never been anyone exactly like you ever before and there never will be anyone exactly like you ever again? That fact alone makes everyone, every living soul—rich or poor, black or white, man or woman— worthy of respect. There is a beautiful old saying in the Jewish religion: 'He who saves one soul, saves the entire world.' It means that everybody is precious— whatever the color of their skin, whatever their religion—everyone has a right to be here."

"That all sounds fine in theory, but it's a little different in practice," said the young man.

"Of course, isn't everything?" replied Millie. "But, that's not to say it can't be done. If I can do it, I'm sure anyone can. It's all a question of finding things to respect about yourself and about others."

"What do you mean?" asked the young man.

"Well, our brains are incredible mechanisms, and even today with the advances of modern medicine, we still know only a fraction of all there is to know about the human brain. One of the incredible facilities that your brain has is to find an answer to any question we put to it. Of course it may find the wrong answer, but it will always find an answer. So, for instance, if you were to ask yourself what things you like and respect about yourself, your brain will come up with answers. In fact, the old Chinese man asked me precisely that question. At first I said there was nothing I respected or liked about myself, and then he said, 'I know, but if there was something, what do you think it would be?' And so I thought about it some more and a few things did come to mind. I knew I had an intelligent mind as I was always top of the class when I had been at school, I respected the fact that I had survived on my own, and despite the desperation of my circumstances, I had never robbed or cheated or hurt anyone. Gradually I began to feel better about myself."

The young man scribbled down some notes and then looked up at Dr. Hopkins. "So, asking yourself what you respect or like about yourself is a way of finding self-respect."

"Well, it certainly helped me. And, if it can help me, it can help anyone. This is because when you ask, 'What do I respect about myself?' your brain will come up with some answers."

"What if there is nothing?"

"There is *always* something, and very often a number of things that will come to mind. For instance, it may be that you respect the fact that you are honest, or that you have a job, or that you do regular physical exercise. It doesn't matter what it is, so long as you can find something that you respect about yourself. It's also a good question to ask yourself about other people, particularly those you tend to dislike."

"Why is that?" asked the young man.

"Because your mind will then focus on the things that you respect about them rather than the things you dislike about them. And, once that happens, you will be more able to willing to treat them lovingly."

"And by lovingly, you mean . . . ?"

"Acting kindly and considerately toward them. You see a lot of people treat others as if they were worthless," continued Dr. Hopkins, "but the truth is we all come from the same Creator, we are all made in God's image. One of the worst mistakes you can make in life is to underestimate the power of one individual. Every individual has the power to change the world, and in his or her own small way each person does change the world. When we respect a person's true worth, we begin to treat them differently.

"I remember when I was sleeping rough on the streets, I awoke one night in a passageway to find a policeman urinating on my face."

"What!" exclaimed the young man. "What on earth did he do that for?"

"He obviously had only contempt for people like me who were homeless," answered Dr. Hopkins. "He had no respect for me as a human being and I will never forget seeing him standing over me, laughing. To him it was a big joke.

"I am convinced that most problems in the world arise because we lose respect—for ourselves, for other people, for life. As a result, we have no love. All over the world you can see the results—Arab and Jew, black and white, Protestant and Catholic—if only we would respect each other's beliefs, we might begin to love each other.

"Once you appreciate your own worth you can begin to appreciate the value of others and respect them. And when you respect someone you can begin to love them. For instance, it was only when I learned to respect myself and to love myself, that I was comfortable being with other people. I found that when I looked for things to respect in other people, my attitude towards them changed and I felt more able to be loving to them.

The young man smiled to himself as he made notes. It seemed so simple, and it made such sense, but he had never really thought about the importance of respect in creating love and loving relationships before.

"But, tell me something," he said. "How did you manage to become a professor from living a life on the streets?"

Dr. Hopkins smiled. "One of the people on the old Chinese man's list turned out to be a nun. She was a wonderful person and did so much to help me; she got me off the streets and found me accommodation at the local convent. The arrangement was that I could stay there, and in return I mucked in with the chores—cooking, gardening, cleaning. Anything and everything. And from day one I was welcomed as one of the sisters, as one of their family. They never saw me as a worthless drunk or low-life; to them I was just a fellow human being who needed help, and they gave it. It was a new experience for me—the first time in my life when I felt as if I was wanted.

"It was also the nun who encouraged me to further my education. She said that I had been blessed with a fine brain and that I should use it. Noone had ever encouraged me like that before and I went back to school attending evening classes. Everyone in the convent encouraged me in my efforts and after seven years I finally achieved a first-class honors degree. The following year I got my masters degree and three years later I was awarded a doctorate. That was the greatest, most memorable, day in my life. All of the sisters from the convent turned up for the ceremony and I will never forget the moment when my name was called and I stepped up to collect my degree. As I was handed my degree, I turned to face the gallery. It was a moment I will cherish for the rest of my life; twenty nuns stood up whistling, clapping and cheering. And then, as I walked off the stage, I saw someone else standing up at the back of the auditorium. It was a little old Chinese man with his hands in the air clapping with a beaming smile on his face."

Later that day, the young man summarized the notes he had made of his meeting with Millie Hopkins:

The second secret of Abundant Love—the power of respect.

You cannot love anyone or anything unless you first respect them.

The first person you need to respect is yourself.

To begin to gain self-respect ask yourself, "What do I respect about myself?"

To gain respect for others, even those you may dislike, ask yourself "What do I respect about them?"

The
POWER
of
GIVING

Mrs. Geraldine Williams' struggle to find happiness and love began when she emerged from her mother's womb with no legs and only one hand. She was one of thousands of babies deformed by the Thalidomide tragedy in the 1960s. A drug which had been given to pregnant women was found to cause the most terrible physical deformities in their babies. The young man couldn't help feeling awkward when, sitting in her wheelchair, Mrs. Williams extended her prosthetic limb to greet him.

"I was so pleased to get your message," said Mrs. Williams, ignoring the young man's awkwardness and leading him into her living room. "It has been over ten years now since I met the old Chinese man, but I can remember it as if it was yesterday." Mrs. Williams motioned for the young man to take a seat on the sofa and she positioned her wheelchair opposite him. "I met him in the park one summer's evening. It was the evening of the college dance. I remember sitting there as the sun was setting thinking that nobody, other than my parents, would ever love me the way I was. I just couldn't imagine anyone ever wanting to take me to a dance. And then I began to cry.

"Suddenly, I heard a man's voice asking me if I was all right. I looked up and there he was . . . an elderly Chinese man standing beside me. He gave me a tissue to wipe my eyes and sat down on the bench next to me. He reached over and touched my arm lightly and said, 'Perhaps I can help you?' 'No one can help me,' I muttered. 'Why not?' he asked. 'There is nothing that can solve my problem,' I said. 'In my country,' he said, 'we believe that every problem brings with it a greater gift that can enrich our lives.' 'There is nothing about my problem that can enrich my life, I can assure you,' I said.

"'I have a friend,' he said, 'a remarkable man. He was riding a motorcycle ten years ago when a truck pulled out in front of him. There was no time to swerve to avoid a collision and all he could do to save his life was to try and skid underneath the truck. He made it too, but as he skidded along the road, the petrol cap popped off and within a split second he was engulfed with flames. He woke up three days later in searing pain and third degree burns covering over 70 percent of his body. His face was disfigured, his fingers burned to stubs and he was paralyzed from the waist down. But he had something many people lack, and that is an indomitable spirit. Even after his wife left him because she didn't want to live with what she called 'a fried cripple', he still managed to continue with his life and he eventually became a millionaire. This was a man who was horribly disfigured, confined to a wheelchair, and he didn't even have any fingers on his hands because they had been burned to stubs. One can hardly imagine a more severe handicap. Nobody believed he would be able to lead a normal life, or be able to have a loving relationship. Surely, they said, he would be bitter, resentful and angry at his fate. After all, what was there left for him to live for? But you know they were all wrong. He never felt angry or bitter or resentful, because he knew that on the inside he was the same person as he always had been. He still had dreams he could follow, and he followed them. He became a very successful businessman and an inspiration to all who knew him. And what is more, he met a woman who he described as the woman of his dreams and he married her!'

"I turned around to face the old Chinese man. 'There really is such a man?' I asked. 'Yes, there is. He is a great inspiration to all who know him. His attitude to life is simple: you can either get busy living or get busy dying, and he wasn't ready to die.'

"It was then that I asked the old man how his friend had managed to find a loving relationship. And the old man said matter-of-factly, 'Like anybody else. He followed the secrets of Abundant Love.'

"That was the first time that I had ever heard of the secrets; ten principles through which anyone—so the old Chinese man claimed—could bring not just love into their lives, but love in abundance."

"It sounds too good to be true," said the young man.

"I thought so too, but they worked for me. And if

they can work for me," said Mrs. Williams, "I think they can work for anyone.

The one secret that had the most dramatic impact on my life was . . . the power of giving."

"Giving?" repeated the young man.

"Yes. Giving is, for me, the most remarkable of all the secrets because it is so simple—if you want to receive love, all you have to do is give it. And the more you give, the more you receive."

"I don't follow you," said the young man taking out his trusted notepad and pen. "Can you give me an example?"

"Of course. If you smile at people, what will they usually do?"

"Smile back," answered the young man.

"And if you hug someone, invariably they will hug you as well. A kind word, a gift, a telephone call, a letter . . . anything to show someone that you care about them will all come back to you multiplied."

"But not everyone will respond in that way," said the young man.

"No. Not everyone, but most people will. Love is like a boomerang, it will always come back to you. Maybe not always from the person to whom you gave it, but it will come back to you nonetheless. And it will come back multiplied.

"But what you always have to remember is that, unlike material possessions and money, we all have an unlimited supply of love to give. We don't lose it when we give it. In fact, the only way we can lose love within us is by not giving it away."

"But trying to love some people is a waste of time and energy," said the young man.

"Why?" asked Mrs. Williams.

"Well, because some people are hateful. It's as if their hearts are empty."

"Let me ask you this," replied Mrs. Williams. "If you had seeds which produced the most wonderful flowering plants and trees, where would you plant them? In beautiful forests or lush green meadows or in empty fields?"

"I'm not sure what you're getting at," said the young man.

"Well, which area needs the seeds the most and in which area would your seeds make the most difference?"

"The empty fields."

"Exactly. And now, if the seeds were love, where would they be most needed? In hearts already full of love or in the hearts of embittered, lonely people?"

"I understand what you're saying," said the young man. "But it is not always that easy."

"It takes no more effort to smile than it does to frown, it takes no more time to offer a friendly or encouraging word than it does to criticize. We can choose to be loving just as easily as we can choose to be unkind or uncaring.

"One of the problems is that many of us don't want to be the first ones to give, we'll give only when we have been given. Love is all too often conditional; we say, 'I will love you if you love me.' We're waiting for someone else to make the first move the whole time. And that's one of the reasons why many people rarely experience love—they're waiting for someone else to love them first. But that's sort of like a musician who says, 'I'll play music only when people start dancing.'

"Real love is unconditional, it asks for nothing in return. I once read a beautiful story about a little girl who desperately needed a bone marrow transplant. Fortunately, her younger brother was a perfect match. The doctors explained to the little boy that his sister would die unless she had new blood. But not any blood, she needed his blood. Without hesitating, the boy agreed to help his older sister. But just before he was given the anesthetic, the little boy looked up at the surgeon and asked, 'Will it hurt when I die?' Not even seven years of age, the little boy thought he was giving *all* of his blood and therefore his life to save his older sister. Now you're unlikely to find a love as pure and as true as the love that little boy had for his sister."

"Yes. But it's easier to love members of your own family, isn't it?" said the young man.

"Not necessarily. Some people not only don't love their own family, they positively hate them."

The young man nodded. He remembered Millie Hopkins who had been despised and neglected as a child and grew up to hate her entire family.

"We are all created by the same God," continued Mrs. Williams. "Inside we are all made of the same blood, the same flesh and bone. We are really all part of one family. And, I think that that is what the essence of love is—the ability to see yourself in others.

"So you see, if you want to experience Abundant Love you must be willing to give love unconditionally, without demands for anything in return. Otherwise it is not love. A gift is not a gift if it is not given freely, and love is not love if it is given with conditions. This is why one of the most wonderful ways to experience the joy of giving and the love it creates is by practicing random acts of kindness."

"What do you mean?" asked the young man.

"Random acts of kindness, giving spontaneously, for no reason other than the joy of giving. Seeing a person in the street looking sad and giving them a bunch of flowers. Or complimenting someone on their appearance or their work. Anything that will surprise someone and bring a smile to their face is a random act of kindness and is guaranteed to spread love. And that love will invariably stay with the person you give it to for the rest of their lives."

The young man jotted down notes. He liked that phrase, "Practice random acts of kindness."

"So you really think that just giving and practicing random acts of kindness helped bring love into your life?" he asked.

"Absolutely. It changed the way I felt about myself. All of my life I had thought of myself as a victim, but through the power of giving I discovered that even though I was crippled, there were plenty of things I could do for other people, and I could make a difference in other people's lives.

"It is a law of human nature—whenever you give love, you receive love at the same time. Have you ever done something for someone because you cared about them without any ulterior motive?"

The young man nodded. "Of course." He remembered a time, only a few weeks back, when he had seen a young mother struggling to push a pram up a flight of stairs. It was rush hour and people were pushing past her. He stopped and helped the woman lift the pram up the stairs.

"How did you feel? You felt good about yourself, right?"

Again the young man nodded. He had felt very good about himself. In fact it was the only evening that he returned home from work not feeling exhausted. It was as if helping the woman had given him energy.

"That is the power of giving," said Mrs. Williams. "And not only does it help you feel love, but it also helps build loving relationships. It is something that never fails. In fact giving is a sure-fire guarantee for life-long happiness and love between two people."

"Why is that?" asked the young man.

"Well it's simply this; if you focus on what you can give in a relationship rather than what you can take, you can't go wrong. All relationships are about give and take, you agree?"

"Yes."

If you want to take more than you want to give, you will inevitably experience problems in any relationship. On the other hand, thinking about what you can give to your partner, you can't go wrong. Before committing to a life-long relationship, most people only consider what their partner will be able to do for them. If they would turn the question around and ask instead 'What will I be able to do for my partner?' they would be focusing on what they can contribute to the relationship rather than simply what they can take from it. And that kind of loving attitude can only help create a loving partnership."

The young man thought about it, and the more he did, the more it made sense to him. He had always thought that love was something you received from other people. It had never occurred to him that you could experience love by giving it. Perhaps this was where he had gone wrong with his past relationships; he had only ever thought about what he wanted from a partner, not what he could give to someone else.

"Let me tell you something quite incredible that happened five years ago. I was watching a television documentary about a drug scandal in Mexico—the Thalidomide drug was still being prescribed 25 years after being banned in Western countries."

"That's outrageous," said the young man shaking his head.

"I know. I couldn't believe my eyes. So many little children so needlessly and so horribly deformed. One young girl particularly caught my attention. She was seven or eight, and like me she was born with no legs, but she also had facial deformities. She had learnt to cope, but she was in great pain every day, and her future looked so bleak.

"She came from a poor family who couldn't afford the medical treatment necessary for her to be able to walk comfortably or the cosmetic surgery she needed on her face. The artificial limbs she had were, apart from being very basic, badly fitted and very uncomfortable. It was painful for her to walk with them and she wasn't able to sit down unless she first took them off. Can you believe that the school bus driver actually refused to allow her to travel on the school bus because she was unable to sit down when wearing her artificial legs?"

The young man shook his head in disbelief.

"I knew there and then that here was someone I had to help. I read once that love is nothing more than the discovery of ourselves in others and delight in the recognition. I never really understood what that meant until that day. I didn't just see a crippled and disadvantaged little girl, I saw myself in her. We had a common bond through our handicaps. For the first time in my life I thought that my own suffering might have had some purpose.

"In the months that followed I began a campaign to raise money to get that little girl a new pair of artificial legs and the necessary physical therapy treatment which would enable her to sit down. I also desperately wanted to help her get the cosmetic surgery to correct her facial deformities. So I organized garden parties, raffles, jumble sales and sought donations from whoever and wherever I could. Eighteen months later, I had just about raised the funds and I also managed to persuade a leading cosmetic surgeon to do the necessary cosmetic surgery free of charge.

"After the treatment and the fitting of her new legs, I went to meet her, and as soon as she saw me, she ran toward me with tears in her eyes and threw her arms around me and cried, 'Thank you. Thank you,' over and over again. That was the first time I experienced love in such abundance that I wept uncontrollably. Never before had I cried such tears of joy as I did holding that little girl in my arms that day.

"It was only then that I began to understand what the old Chinese man had meant when he asked me: 'Who is more handicapped? A person who cannot walk or talk, or hear or see, or a person who is unable to laugh, and to cry, and to love?' I realized for the first time that, even in my crippled physical state, inside I was really no different than anybody else. And on that day I knew that despite my own difficulties and regardless of the sham and drudgery in the world, when we fill our hearts with love, life can be so beautiful.

"A year later I met a man—a kind, gentle, wonderful man. He was a social worker at the local community center I attended. We hit it off immediately, I don't know what it was, but something clicked. We soon became close friends, and then a few months later the miracle I had dreamed of actually happened . . . he invited me to a dance!

"A year later we were married and we now have two beautiful children. So you see the old Chinese man was right—every problem does bring with it a greater gift that can enrich your life. As long as you are able to give of yourself, as long as you have something to contribute, you are able to find love."

Later that evening, the young man read over the notes he had made in his meeting with Mrs. Williams:

The third secret of Abundant Love—the power of giving.

If you want to receive love, all you have to do is give it!

The more love you give, the more you will receive.

To love is to give of yourself, freely and unconditionally.

Practice random acts of kindness.

Before committing to a relationship ask not what

the other person will be able to give to you, but rather what will you be able to give to them.

The secret formula of a happy, lifelong, loving relationship is to always focus on what you can give instead of what you can take.

The *POWER* of *FRIENDSHIP*

The fourth person on the young man's list was a man by the name of William Bachman. Mr. Bachman was a free-lance journalist whose articles regularly appeared in the national press and who had also written a best-selling book entitled *Friends and Lovers*. He was a tall, slim man with pointed, angular features, but his face beamed with pleasure when he welcomed the young man at his home.

"The secrets of Abundant Love," confided Mr. Bachman, "completely changed my life. I spent over ten years searching in vain to find that one special relationship, someone to share my life, and there was a time when I thought it was just never going to happen. But, within a year of learning the secrets of Abundant Love, not only had I found the woman of my dreams, but all of my relationships with my family and friends were transformed."

"In what way?" asked the young man.

"Well all of my relationships seemed to become closer, stronger."

The young man looked incredulous. "The secrets had that big an impact on your life?" he asked.

Mr. Bachman smiled. "Most definitely. I know it sounds all a bit too fantastical, but once you try them you will see that they really do work.

"Although all of the secrets helped me in their different ways, the one which I think I most needed to learn was . . . the power of friendship."

"The power of friendship?" repeated the young man. "What exactly do you mean?"

"Well, I used to think that love was about romance between two people, and don't get me wrong, it is. But it is also much more. It is about caring, it is about being there when someone needs you, that's why real love is more than just romance, it is about friendship."

The young man took out his notebook and began to write notes as Mr. Bachman continued. "Like many other people, I searched everywhere I could to find someone to love. I went to singles bars, I went to parties and nightclubs, and although I met and dated plenty of women, I never met the right woman. I was beginning to think I would never find anyone. I remember sitting alone in a bar in the center of town one evening and the next thing I knew, a little old Chinese man was sitting beside me.

"He raised his glass and said, 'hello,' and I raised mine back. We started talking. He asked me if I was married. I told him, 'no.' 'Girlfriend?' he asked. Again I said, 'no.' 'Why?' he asked. I told him, 'Because I haven't met the right girl yet?' And then he said something that made me think about my situation more seriously, he said, 'Perhaps you're looking for her in the wrong places!'"

"Wrong places?" repeated the young man. "What are the wrong places?"

"My reaction precisely," said Mr. Bachman. "I told him I went to bars and nightclubs where there were plenty of single women. He looked at me in utter astonishment and then broke out into a fit of laughter. I asked him what was so funny and he asked, 'Have you ever found a date in a bar or a nightclub?'

"'A few,'" I replied, but when he questioned me further I had to admit that none of them had lasted for more than a few weeks."

"What is wrong with going to bars or nightclubs to meet people?" asked the young man.

"Nothing at all," said Mr. Bachman. "Sometimes you might get lucky, but as the old Chinese man said to me, if it's a lasting relationship and love you're after, a dimly-lit, smoke-filled room with so much noise that you have to shout just to be heard probably isn't the best place to find it."

"Then what is the best place?" persisted the young man, who frequently went to bars and nightclubs in the hope of meeting women.

"Well, that depends upon you."

"What do you mean?"

"Well, as the old man explained to me, 'If you want to find true love, you must first find a true friend.' It is so simple, yet I had never thought of it before. We often assume that a strong physical attraction is the primary requirement for love. Now I'm not saying that physical attraction is not important in a loving relationship, but if we want love in abundance—if we want love that will last us a lifetime—we must look beyond people's outward appearances.

"Real love is rooted not in physical attraction, but in friendship. Or as the French writer Antoine de Saint Exupéry said, 'Love does not consist of gazing at each other, but looking outward together in the same direction.' It is even written in the Bible that 'Two people cannot journey together unless they agree.' Common beliefs, shared goals and interests, mutual respect and admiration are the foundation of a lasting, loving relationship."

"Is it really that important?" asked the young man looking up from his notepad.

"There is no doubt about it. In fact a team of sociologists at an American university demonstrated just how important friendship is to a loving relationship. They asked hundreds of married couples who were still happily living together after fifty years or more what they attributed their success to, and their answers showed a predominant common factor . . . friendship. Every person had said that their partner was their best friend. They all had common beliefs and common interests, common goals and a common direction in life. Everything else including physical beauty and material possessions was, in the long term, irrelevant. The thing that binds lifelong, loving relationships is friendship.

"This is what first inspired me to write my book *Friends and Lovers*. Many people still make the mistake of believing love springs from physical attraction, but our looks are ephemeral, they fade with each passing day.

"Conversely, love rooted in friendship and respect grows stronger each day. After all, how beautiful is a woman who lies and cheats, and how attractive is a man who beats his girlfriend?

"So you see instead of focusing solely on physical attraction for your relationships, it would be better instead to seek partners who share your beliefs, your values and your goals."

The young man nodded in agreement. He instinctively knew it made sense. Since his meeting with Dr. Puchia one of the things he had written down about his ideal partner was that she would have to share his love of the outdoors.

"I see your point," said the young man. "But you still have to find that friend, don't you?"

"That's true," answered Mr. Bachman. "But to have friends, all you have to do is be friendly. To have special friends, you have to be friendly with people who share your interests and beliefs."

"That's easier said than done," said the young man.

"Why? What hobbies or activities do you like doing?"

"Well, I like to go hiking on the weekends, and sailboarding. And I like going to the opera."

"So where do you think you are more likely to make friends; in a smoke-filled bar or in a hiking club, a sailboarding group or the local operatic society?"

"I understand what you're saying," replied the young man. "But what about those people who have no real hobbies or interests?"

"They ought to think about finding some interests or hobbies that they enjoy. Things that they are passionate about; it doesn't matter what it is—it could be a sport like football, tennis, swimming or cycling, or a more social activity like dancing, drama or hiking, or even a political cause. Once we find things that interest us, it is easy finding other people who share our interests because we have something in common. If you have nothing in common with another person it is unlikely that you will be able to maintain a close relationship with them."

"When you put it that way it sounds so simple."

"It is simple, yet at the same time, it is something we often overlook. People are far too concerned with finding a partner, a husband or a wife, when if they instead looked to build friendships, they would find that loving relationships would follow."

"But just because you are friends with someone, it doesn't mean to say you will find them attractive and develop a loving relationship," said the young man.

"No. You are absolutely right, it doesn't. But if you're not friends, your relationship is unlikely to last."

"But there are times, aren't there, when two people fall in love—or rather they are physically attracted to each other—and only later become friends."

"Yes. Of course, that's possible," admitted Mr. Bachman, "and not uncommon. The essential point is that friendship is a vital element of any life-long, loving relationship because it is a vital part of loving.

"That is why one of the best questions you can ask yourself when considering whether a person is the right one for you to share your life with is—'Is she my best friend?' If the answer is 'no' you ought to think very carefully before committing to that person for the rest of your life."

The young man jotted down some notes and then looked up. "What about people who are already in a committed relationship?" he asked. "I suppose it is too late for them to start considering the power of friendship."

"Not at all," answered Mr. Bachman. "Many relationships have been saved by the power of friendship. Friendship can be built, all you need is simply to find common ground, shared interests, things you can do together. Two people can become friends again and rebuild their relationship because invariably when our friendship grows, so too do our feelings of love."

"One last thing," said the young man, just as he was leaving. "Did you ever meet the girl of your dreams?"

Mr. Bachman smiled. "Of course," he said. "And I married her. I met Rachel at a hiking club. I wasn't physically attracted to her at first, and neither I think was she particularly attracted to me, but as we got to know each other things started to change. We felt so comfortable being with each other; she was the first woman to whom I could talk about the things that mattered to me. We discovered that we shared so many interests and had such similar beliefs, it was as if we were soul mates. We became very close friends and then one day I realized that I was in love with her and wanted to share my life with her."

When the young man got home he read over the notes he had made in his meeting with Mr. Bachman:

The fourth secret of Abundant Love—the power of friendship.

To find a true love, you must first find a true friend.

Love does not consist of gazing into each other's eyes, but rather looking outward together in the same direction.

To love someone completely you must love them for who they are, not what they look like.

Friendship is the soil through which love's seeds grow.

If you want to bring love into a relationship, you must first bring friendship.

The
POWER
of
TOUCH

The following morning the young man arrived at the city hospital to meet the next person on his list, a Dr. Peter Young. Dr. Young was the chief surgeon at the hospital. He was a tall, handsome black man with cropped jet black hair and deep, dark brown eyes. As the young man entered his office, Dr. Young rose from his chair behind his desk and greeted the young man with a gentle, but firm handshake. "Hi, it's great to meet you," said Dr. Young.

"Likewise," said the young man. "Thanks for taking the time to see me."

"Oh, it's my pleasure," said Dr. Young, motioning for the young man to take a seat. "Can I get you a drink?"

"Do you have a mint tea?" asked the young man.

"Coming right up," said Dr. Young as he opened the door and asked his secretary for a pot of tea for two.

"Now tell me again," asked Dr. Young, "exactly when and how did you meet the old Chinese man?" As the young man finished telling his story, the tea was brought in. Dr. Young handed the young man a cup. "I met the old man 15 years ago," he said. "I had only just qualified as a surgeon and I knew it all—at least I thought I did. As far as I was concerned, my job was to cut patients open, remove the problem and sew them back up again. I was pretty good at it too, but I never once sat at a patient's bedside."

"Really? Why?" asked the young man.

"Because I considered it a waste of my time to sit and talk to patients. That was a job for the nurses. I even chastised student doctors if they spent too much time with patients. I know it sounds ridiculous but I was always taught that a good surgeon's skill lay in his hands. It took a very special old Chinese man to help me understand that I was wrong—a good surgeon's skill does not lie in his hands . . . it lies in his heart."

The young man listened intently as Dr. Young continued, "I was doing my early morning rounds one day. There was nothing unusual that morning until I entered the room of a patient and found a ward orderly sitting beside her, holding her hand. 'Shouldn't you be doing your job?' I told him. As he slowly turned to face me, I will never forget his expression. Those dark brown eyes looked directly at me as he answered. 'Yes. But as you are not doing yours, somebody must do it for you.'

"Needless to say, I lost my temper. 'Now you listen to me . . . ' I said, but before I could finish, he raised his hand and whispered, 'Not now, please. This lady needs help.'

"I was incensed. 'How dare a ward orderly speak to me like that,' I thought. This particular woman had terminal cancer. We had found that she had an inoperable tumor in her brain. 'She is going to . . . ' I said but before I could finish the sentence, the old man raised his hand again and said once more 'Not now, please. Not now.'

"I waited outside the room ready to give him a piece of my mind, but when he came outside, he looked straight into my eyes and said 'She will live, Doctor.' 'What do you mean, she will live?' I demanded. 'She has an inoperable brain tumor.' 'Have you never witnessed a patient recovering from an illness when you thought they would die?' he asked. 'Yes, of course,' I replied. 'But . . . ' 'What do you think brings about those recoveries?' 'I haven't got the slightest idea,' I answered impatiently. 'They are freak happenings.' 'No doctor," he said. 'They are miracles! And what produces those miracles? Love! Love,' he said, 'is the most powerful healing force in the entire Universe, more powerful than any medicine. Without love a surgeon is a mechanic, not a doctor.'

"And then he handed me a piece of paper and said, 'If you want to learn how to be a doctor, you need to meet these people.' I looked at it and all it contained was a list of ten people and their phone numbers, but when I looked back up the old man had disappeared.

"I was so outraged by what the old man had said that I went directly to the administrator's office to try and locate the old man and give him a piece of my mind. But they had no record of a Chinese man working in our department. At first I thought there must have been a mix up with the records—there sometimes is, a computer error or something—but there was no record anywhere of an old Chinese man fitting my description, so I let it go . . . until the next day."

"What happened?" asked the young man.

"I was called by the ward sister to come immediately . . . the woman with the inoperable brain tumor was sitting up, her appetite regained and she said she was feeling much better. I couldn't believe my eyes; here was someone who had been suffering from nausea and dizziness for months and only two days earlier had had brain surgery. She even thanked me and said the operation must have gone well. It was unbelievable, a miracle! I couldn't imagine what the old Chinese man had done for this woman, but I knew that he must have done something. The only way I could think of to find out more about him was to contact the people on the list he had given me.

"Of course, all of the people had met the old Chinese man and they talked about the secrets of Abundant Love. I had never heard of these secrets before, and naturally I was very sceptical but, at the same time, I was curious to find out more about how the old man had managed to help my patient. I had never considered the relevance of love in health and healing; after all, at medical school we weren't taught that there was any connection between love or affection and our healing mechanisms. But there is. The old man was absolutely right, love is the strongest healing force."

"Really?" said the young man.

"Yes. And there have been research studies to

prove it. For instance, studies have shown that people who enjoy happy, loving relationships have less than ten percent the rate of serious diseases as people who do not, and healing has been shown to be much faster and more successful in patients who feel loved."

"That's incredible," said the young man.

"It is, isn't it," said Dr. Young. "And very exciting for people like me who are involved in the healing professions.

"As I learned about these secrets of Abundant Love I gradually noticed changes in my own life."

"In what way?" asked the young man.

"Well, in all sorts of ways. My relationships with my family and friends improved, I started to get along much better with my girlfriend, but perhaps the greatest difference came in my job. I started to see patients as people, not just case numbers, but what was most remarkable, especially in the field of medicine, was one secret in particular ... the power of touch."

"What has touch got to do with love?" asked the young man.

"There is unbelievable power in touch. It bonds people and breaks down barriers in a way that nothing else can do, and we all respond to it. Touch has an energy that produces miracles.

"Not so long ago, researchers conducted an interesting experiment at a teaching hospital in London. What happened was this: the chief surgeon would usually visit each of his patients the night before their operation to answer any questions they may have and to explain to them the general nature of the operation. But on this occasion the surgeon held each patient's hand for the few minutes that he spoke to them. Would you believe that those patients recovered on average three times faster than other patients!

"You see when we touch someone in a caring manner both our and their physiologies begin to change—stress hormones reduce, the nervous system relaxes, our immune system improves and it even affects our emotions and moods as well.

"When I learned all of this I started a 'touch' program in hospital wards. All of the carers were encouraged to touch, hold hands or hug patients. It was so successful that it spread to the psychiatric wards. I remember one patient, a young boy, who had cerebral palsy and who was confined to a wheelchair. When I met him I knelt down and gave him a hug and suddenly he tried to speak, his eyes filled with tears and he squeezed me back. The staff said it was the first time in three years that the boy had responded to anyone."

"That is remarkable," said the young man.

Dr. Young smiled. "The psychology department was so intrigued with the power of touch that they arranged another experiment a few years ago out on the high street. They got a woman to stand by the telephone booth and ask passers-by if they could give her the right change. Very few people offered to help her. Then the same woman began to touch a person's arm as she asked them for help, and lo and behold most of the people she asked—male and female—willingly agreed to help her.

"So you can see why touching, hugging and holding hands are so important if we want to give and receive love. It changes us physically, mentally and emotionally. This is why touch is so important if we want to give and receive love in abundance."

The young man nodded and looked away briefly, thinking about how little physical contact he had with his family and friends. Very little touching or hugging. He would usually give his mother a peck on the cheek when they met, and his father offered him a handshake, but there was no real warmth or affection.

"Touching or hugging is not easy," he said, turning back to Dr. Young.

"Why?" replied Dr. Young. "All you have to do is open your arms. Anyone can do it."

"Yes, but you don't know how someone will respond. They might reject you, they could even be hostile."

"Even more reason for you to try to break down their barriers. Remember love requires courage. You have to be willing to risk rejection and pain, but most of the time you will win. People will open up to you. If we all waited for others to make the first move, where would we be?

"All you have to do is open your arms to people, and you will find that it opens your heart. Then you will experience the energy of love sparked by the power of touch."

Later that evening the young man read over his notes:

The fifth secret of Abundant Love—the power of touch.

Touch is one of the most powerful expressions of

love, breaking down barriers and bonding relationships.

Touch changes our physical and emotional states and makes us more receptive to love.

Touch can help heal the body and warm the heart.

When you open your arms, you open your heart.

The
POWER
of
LETTING
GO

Two days later the young man sat in a small café in the center of town opposite the sixth person on his list, a woman by the name of Judith Renshaw.

Mrs. Renshaw was a young woman in her early thirties, married with two young children. She was quite a tall, well-built woman, by no stretch of the imagination could she be considered a classical beauty, but she had pretty facial features—large hazel eyes, a small turned-up nose and a disarming smile.

"I first heard about the secrets of Abundant Love eleven years ago," she said to the young man. "I was going through a difficult time; my boyfriend and I had only recently separated after seeing each other for the best part of a year. When he told me that he thought we should stop seeing each other I was completely devastated. I couldn't eat or sleep, I couldn't concentrate at work, I lost so much weight that some people didn't even recognize me. Even after a month had passed, I still found it hard to accept that the relationship was over.

"Then one day I was sitting on a bench in the church square and an old Chinese man came and sat down next to me. He took a small paper bag out of his pocket and began to feed the pigeons. The pigeons flocked around him, pecking at the pieces of bread he threw for them. Pretty soon there were hundreds of them. He turned to me and said hello. 'Do you like pigeons?' he asked. I shrugged my shoulders. 'Not particularly,' I replied. 'But I can see you that you do.'

"He smiled. 'When I was a young boy,' he said, 'there was a man in my village who bred pigeons. The man was very proud of his birds and would often tell his friends how much he loved them. But one day, when the man was showing his pigeons to me and a group of other children, I just couldn't understand why, if he loved his birds, he kept them in cages unable to spread their wings and fly. So I asked him, and he replied, 'If they were not in cages, they might fly away and leave me.' But I still didn't understand. How can you love something and keep it caged against its will? 'In my country we have a saying,' he said, 'if you love something, set it free. If it comes back to you, it is yours; if it doesn't, it never was yours.'"

The young man took out his pen and notepad and began to make notes as Mrs. Renshaw continued.

"I had the strangest feeling that there was a special message in the old man's story for me. I don't know why, after all, he couldn't possibly have known my predicament. But the story was too close to my own situation for comfort. I was trying to force my boyfriend to come back to me. I had always thought that everything would be all right so long as my boyfriend stayed with me. I suppose, looking back, I just didn't want to be alone. But that isn't love, is it? It's just a fear of loneliness.

"The old man turned away and continued feeding the pigeons. After a few minutes contemplating what he had just said, I said that sometimes it is not easy to let go of someone you love. He nodded. 'But,' he said, 'if you cannot let them be free, you are not loving them.' We talked about it for a little while and it was then that he mentioned the secrets of Abundant Love. It sounded too incredible to me, I had always thought that love was either part of your fate in life or it wasn't.

"I couldn't believe that love and loving relationships were things that we had any control over. It was only later that I understood that we write the pages in the book of Life. Destiny is not so much governed by the stars, but by our thoughts, our decisions and our actions.

"For instance, I had always imagined that I would experience the joys of love when I found a loving relationship. But I had it back to front: it is when we experience the joys of love that we create loving relationships.

"Just before the old man left, he gave me a piece of paper . . . " continued Mrs. Renshaw.

"Containing a list of ten names and phone numbers?" interrupted the young man.

Mrs. Renshaw smiled. "Of course. I contacted each of them in turn and gradually learned more about the secrets of Abundant Love. And the amazing thing was, they really did work."

"In what way?" asked the young man.

"Well, I think just by understanding that I could change things, that I was in control rather than a victim of fate helped enormously.

"All of them helped me in one way or another but the one that I think helped me the most, especially at that time in my life, was . . . the power of letting go.

"Love cannot be forced. We have to let the people we love be free, otherwise we are no better than the pigeon breeder. If we love someone we must allow them to be free. Free to make their own decisions, free to live their life the way they want to, not the way we want them to."

It is not always the easiest thing in the world to let someone you love go, but there is no other way. If you don't, you'll end up bitter, angry and depressed. But I am not just talking about letting go at the end of a relationship, we also need to let go when we are *within* a relationship."

"What do you mean?" asked the young man. "If you're in a relationship, why would you want to let go of the other person?"

"Because we all need space. People need to be free within a relationship otherwise they will soon feel trapped. If we truly love someone, we must respect their wishes and their needs.

"When we cling on to someone, we can emotionally suffocate them, and it is generally out of jealousy, insecurity or fear that we do it, not love."

"So by letting go you mean letting a person be free," said the young man.

"Yes. Although there is a little more to it than that. It is not just physical attachments that we need to let go of; we must let go of anything and everything that is an obstacle to love."

"Such as?" asked the young man.

"Well, for instance, we must let go of our prejudices and our judgements about people."

"I'm not sure that I understand," said the young man, looking up from his notepad.

"Well, if we have any prejudices against a person or a class of people, it will inevitably affect our behavior toward them. We are hardly likely to be loving toward a person if we insist on holding onto prejudices. To be prejudiced is to judge someone even before we know them. Most prejudices are false anyway, ridiculous generalizations about a class of people. It's incredible when you think about it, how many prejudices people have."

"Such as . . . ?"

"Such as, 'all black men are criminals' or 'all Irish people are stupid' or 'all women are bad drivers' or 'all Jewish people are misers' or 'all gentiles are anti-semitic.' It's all nonsense! And it prevents us from being loving.

"Another thing we need to let go of is our ego. Few people realize that their ego is one of the biggest obstacles to Abundant Love."

"In what way?" asked the young man.

"How many people do you know who have had raging arguments about trivial matters? Even though the subject of disagreement may be totally inconsequential, they'll still argue to the bitter end, even to the point where they have forgotten what they are arguing about! They would prefer to prove a point even at the expense of ruining their relationship."

"But sometimes, you have to put the other person straight, don't you?" said the young man. "If they are wrong about something, they should be told."

"I'm not saying that there are not times to state your case," replied Mrs. Renshaw, "especially about matters which are important to you, but if it's of no real consequence who is right, then why waste time and energy arguing. What do you possibly have to gain other than proving that you are right and the other person is wrong? What you have to ask yourself is, does it really matter what the other person believes? And, is it worth damaging this relationship to prove my point? If the answer to those questions is 'no', why bother arguing?"

The young man could see the logic. It was so simple. He cringed as he thought about the amount of times he had argued with friends and acquaintances over inconsequential trivia.

"There is a saying," continued Mrs. Renshaw, "that in life sometimes you have to choose between being loved and being right. You can put your efforts into trying to win an argument or trying to win love. If love is your priority, you don't need to prove that somebody else is wrong and you are right about trivial things. You can let it go.

"Remember, if we want love, we have to let go of anything and everything that is an obstacle to love. Our ego is only one of them. I think the most important things we need to let go of are anger, resentment and bitterness."

"But how do you let go of anger or resentment?" asked the young man.

"In one word: Forgiveness. If you want to experience Abundant Love, you must be able to forgive because there is not enough room in anyone's heart for hate and love to live together."

"But isn't it better to get even, take revenge. An eye for an eye, and a tooth for a tooth."

"If we all followed that philosophy, the whole world would be filled with blind and toothless people. There is simply not enough room in a human heart for hatred and love to live side by side. Resentment destroys your spirit, whereas forgiveness frees the soul to love.

"Noone on this earth can claim to be perfect, but through learning to forgive we can have perfect relationships. We all make mistakes and if we want people to forgive us, we have to be willing to forgive them as well. Even the most hardened criminal started life as an innocent baby. Who is to say that, if we had such a person's upbringing, we would have been any better?"

Of course, letting go is only one of ten secrets and they are all important, but the power of letting go helps us to keep loving at times when it is most needed."

"But surely you are not suggesting that people should try and suppress their anger or fears?" said the young man.

"Of course not," said Mrs. Renshaw. "Anger, fear, resentment are all natural human emotions and they have their place. All I am saying is that if we want to experience love, we must be willing to let go of the negative emotions. If we hold on to them, it is like creating a self-imposed emotional prison which prevents us from loving.

"The power of letting go didn't just help me get over the emotional pain of a broken relationship all those years ago, it helped me through many difficult times later on in my life. I remember the day my father died in the hospital. He was in the final stages of cancer and in great pain. It was the saddest day of my life, I desperately didn't want him to die, but I didn't want him to suffer either. I knew in my heart that sometimes love means letting go."

Later that evening, the young man sat down and read through his notes. Memories came flooding back; his parents' separation when he was only six years old, and the failed relationships of the past few years. He had realized after his meeting with the old Chinese man that he had a fear of being alone as well as a fear of committing to a relationship. He couldn't go on like this, carrying the pain of the past. It was time to let go of the pain and the fear and begin each day afresh. But how? He looked back over the notes he had made during his meeting with Dr. Puchia and found one way to overcome the past and the negative subconscious beliefs we acquire—affirmations! And it was then, as if by some miracle, an affirmation suddenly came into his head: "Today I let go of all my fears, the past has no power over me—today is the beginning of a new life."

He wrote the affirmation down at the bottom of the notes he had made about his meeting with Mrs. Renshaw, and then re-read them one more time:

The sixth secret of Abundant Love—the power of letting go.

If you love something, let it free. If it comes back to you it's yours, if it doesn't it never was.

Even in a loving relationship, people need their own space.

If we want to learn to love, we must first learn to forgive and let go of past hurts and grievances.

Love means letting go of our fears, prejudices, egos and conditions.

"Today I let go of all my fears, the past has no power over me—today is the beginning of a new life."

The POWER of COMMUNICATION

"One of the biggest problems for most people is not that they are unable to love, but that they are unable to express and communicate their love. If we want to experience love and if we want to create loving relationships, we must be willing to communicate our feelings. It was certainly my biggest problem. That is why one of the greatest secrets of Abundant Love is, for me, the power of communication."

The young man was sitting opposite the seventh person on his list, a man by the name of Chris Palmer. Mr. Palmer was a licensed taxi driver—a short, slim man with silver-gray hair and pale, blue eyes—who looked to be around fifty years. It was midday and the two men sat together on a street bench alongside a taxi rank eating sandwiches.

"The amazing thing was that I didn't even realize that I had a problem until I met the old Chinese man," said Mr. Palmer. "I was actually on my way home late one night when he waved me down. He asked if I could take him to the train station as he needed to catch the 11:20 to York. Although it was a little out of my way, I agreed to take him there. We started talking, not about anything in particular, just the usual things—the news, weather, sports. But somehow we got onto the subject of human relationships and love. I told him not to talk to me about love, my wife and I were going through a difficult time and I didn't want to think about it. And it was then that he said something that made a lasting impression on me. He said, "One of the greatest diseases afflicting humankind is the inability to communicate with each other."

"Naturally I asked him to explain himself and he turned to me and said, 'I know a man who couldn't remember the last time he told his wife that he loved her. He couldn't even remember the last time he thanked her for the things she does for him. This man thinks of himself as a man with great strength, but he doesn't even have the courage to tell his wife that he loves her. Can you imagine that?'

"I could imagine it because his description would have fitted me exactly. 'But I'm sure his wife knows that he loves her,' I said.

"Maybe she does, and maybe she doesn't," he answered. "Maybe she needs to be reminded every once in a while. You wouldn't believe the difference it makes to hear someone say, 'thank you', or tell you that they love you. It's part of human nature, we all need to feel appreciated.'

"I said that I had never thought about it like that

before. He looked at me and said, 'It is one of the secrets of Abundant Love . . . the power of communication.'

"I would have asked him to explain, but just then we arrived at the station. The old man got out, turned to me and said, 'Thank you for the ride. You did an excellent job. It was a pleasure being driven by you.' I was stunned. In all my years of driving a taxi, no one had ever thanked me with such feeling or complimented me on my driving. And then he paid me and said, 'Thank you again.' But when I counted the money, I found that he had paid me double the fare. I called out to him and shouted that he had overpaid me, and he turned and smiled and said, 'No, I didn't,' and then turned back and walked on.

"It was then that I looked down at the money and found a note headed 'Secrets of Abundant Love' followed by a list of ten names and telephone numbers. I jumped out of the taxi and ran after the old man as I thought it might be important to him. I went into the station and straight to the information kiosk to find out what platform the 11:20 to York was departing from, hoping that I might be able to catch him. The information officer checked his timetable and then told me that I must have got it wrong; there was no 11:20 to York! 'In fact,' he said, 'the next train to York isn't until the morning.'

"The following day I telephoned all of the people on the old man's list and was surprised to find out that they knew all about the old man and the secrets of Abundant Love. Over the following weeks I met each of the people on the list in turn and learned more about the secrets. I was very skeptical at the time, but they really did work. They made a real difference, particularly the power of communication.

"Did you know, for example, that when people who are having problems with their relationships are asked what they think the cause of their problems are, they all give the same answer: we can't communicate. And it's true; we don't tell each other how we feel, we don't listen to what others are really trying tell us. A lot of people don't even talk at mealtimes, and instead sit and eat in front of the television. If this happens day in, day out, we stop really communicating, and consequently, we stop really loving."

The young man wrote down some notes as Mr. Palmer continued. "If we want to learn to love, we must first learn to communicate, which is something I was never very good at. I kept my problems to myself and rarely shared my feelings. The day after I met the old man I decided to tell my wife that I loved her. I couldn't even remember the last time I had said those three words to her. I tried several times but, for some reason, the words just wouldn't come out. Finally, I took a deep breath and just blurted it out: 'I love you.' My wife looked at me almost as if she was in shock. In fact, she was so taken aback that she asked me to repeat what I had said. This time it was easier. Tears came to her eyes and she threw her arms around me and said, 'I love you too.'

"It felt so good that, even though it was late in the evening, I called my son who was at college to tell him that I loved him. I don't think I had said those three words to him since he was a child. He answered the phone and I said, 'Simon, I just called to tell you that I love you. I thought it was about time I let you know.'

There was silence at the other end and then he said, 'Dad, have you been drinking? Do you know what time it is here?' I had forgotten that he was two hours ahead of us. I said, 'I'm sorry to have woken you up, son. I'm perfectly sober, I just wanted to let you know that I love you.' And then he said, 'I did know Dad, but it's nice to hear it just the same. And by the way, I love you too. Now, can I get some sleep?'

"Some people would say it is ridiculous to think that three words can make such a difference, but they obviously haven't tried saying them."

The young man took a deep breath. He was one of those people. He just couldn't say those words even to his own mother and certainly never to a friend.

"If we can't communicate and express our feelings," continued Mr. Palmer, "we can't give or receive love. The more I thought about it, the more I began to realize just how important it is. I examined my own behavior and found that, not only did I never tell anyone I loved them, but I rarely gave compliments or told people how much I appreciated them. My wife had done my washing and ironing for over twenty years and I had never once said thank you.

"And do you know an amazing thing happened; as soon as I started to express my feelings and let my wife and those around me know how much I appreciated them and cared for them, their behavior toward me changed. They began telling me how much they loved and appreciated me, and before I knew it, all of my relationships had changed and all because I had begun to communicate openly and honestly."

"You mentioned earlier that you never shared your problems," said the young man. "Is that important?"

"Yes. I'm glad you reminded me. Love means sharing and communicating. But this is not just limited to how you feel about someone else, but to your hopes and fears and problems. If you keep all your feelings locked up inside, not only will you tend to become insular and depressed, but you will also be denying the people close to you the opportunity to offer help or sympathy or support in some way."

The young man recalled the old Chinese man's words: "Every problem brings with it a gift that can enrich your life." Mrs. Williams had said the same thing. Perhaps there really is some truth in it, he thought.

"There is no doubt in my mind," continued Mr. Palmer, "that if people want to experience love and improve their relationships, they must learn to communicate. People need to feel appreciated in order to feel loved. One of the most important discoveries I made was that love is not a fixed object. People often assume that once you love someone then that is it, they are set for a lifetime of happiness. But the truth is that love is never static, it is like a plant, it either grows and blossoms or it withers and dies. It all depends upon what we do about it. Communication is the water, without it the plant cannot survive."

The young man looked away as he thought about the times when he had been too frightened to tell the people he loved how much he cared about them.

"I understand what you're saying," said the young man as he turned back to Mr. Palmer, "but how do you learn to communicate, especially if you've never been good at it?"

"I was never a good communicator myself, which

is of course why learning the power of communication helped my relationships so much," said Mr. Palmer. "But I assure you that anyone can learn to communicate. What you need to do is overcome your fears. Some people are afraid they will sound silly or that the other person will reject them. One of the best pieces of advice I was given was to always bear in mind one question: 'If you were about to die and were able to make a telephone call to whoever you wished, who would you call, what would you say . . . and why are you waiting?'

"Always remember that each time you see someone, it could be the last. So, tell them the things you want to tell them while you can. One of the worst pains in life is the pain of regret for not having told someone how you felt about them or how important they are to you, before they died.

"And we need to communicate to prevent problems building up in a relationship. In fact, most problems in relationships stem from the inability of either or both partners to communicate their thoughts and feelings to each other. As a result, resentment and anger build up and eventually someone's temper explodes. If we learn to communicate, small grievances can be dealt with whilst they are still small and relatively insignificant. This means learning to express ourselves to those we love, and also being able to listen to what other people tell us about their feelings. People hear what somebody says to them, but often they don't listen to what is being said.

"And of course if we don't communicate our feelings," explained Mr. Palmer, "we can't even establish a relationship. I mean, you would find it difficult to date a girl if you didn't ask her out, wouldn't you?"

The young man nodded and then looked away. How many opportunities had he let slip, fearing to communicate his feelings?

"You okay?" asked Mr. Palmer after a moment of silence while the young man stared vacantly across the street.

"Yes. I'm fine. Just thinking," replied the young man, returning his attention to Mr. Palmer.

"You know," said Mr. Palmer, "when we learn to communicate and to openly and honestly share our experiences and feelings, life changes. It's like the story of the man who was lost in a forest."

"What's that?" said the young man.

"Well, this particular man was lost in a forest and although he had tried several footpaths, hoping each time that it would lead him out of the forest, they had all led him back to where he started.

"There were a number of paths still left to try and the man, tired and hungry, sat down to consider which path to try next. As he was pondering over his decision, he saw another traveler walking towards him. He called out to the approaching traveler, 'Can you help me? I am lost.' The other man sighed with relief. 'I am lost too.' As they related their experiences to each other, it became apparent that, between them, they had travelled down many of the paths. They were able to help each other avoid following the wrong paths that one or the other had already followed. Soon they were laughing about their journeys and, forgetting their tiredness and hunger, walked through the forest together.

"Life is like the forest; sometimes we get lost and confused, but if we share our experiences and our feelings with others, the journey doesn't seem so bad and sometimes we find better paths, better ways."

That evening the young man read over the notes he had made that day:

The seventh secret of Abundant Love—the power of communication.

When we learn to communicate openly and honestly, life changes.

To love someone is to communicate with them.

Let the people you love know that you love them and appreciate them. Never be afraid to say those three magic words: "I Love You."

Never let an opportunity pass to praise someone.

Always leave someone you love with a loving word—it could be the last time you see them.

If you were about to die but could make telephone calls to the people you loved, who would you call, what would you say and . . . why are you waiting?

The
POWER
of
COMMITMENT

The following day the young man had a meeting arranged with the eighth person on his list. Stanley Conran was the head teacher of a large school situated in a downtrodden part of the inner city, depressed by high crime rates and unemployment. Buildings in the area were run down, shops boarded up and pavements littered with rubbish. It was certainly not an area the young man would have chosen to work or live in. Yet when he arrived at the school and entered through the school gates, he had the impression that he was walking into a different world. The clean pathways passing between immaculately cut lawns and colorful flowerbeds were a stark contrast to the general decay in the surrounding area.

The young man was shown into Mr. Conran's office as he arrived. Mr. Conran, a large, portly man with thick rimmed spectacles that made his eyes look small in relation to his face, rose from his chair and warmly greeted the young man.

"You found your way okay?" he said.

"No problem at all," answered the young man.

"Please sit down," said Mr. Conran. "So tell me, when was it that you met the old Chinese man?"

"A few weeks ago," replied the young man. "Who exactly is he?"

"I really don't know who he is or where he comes from. All I do know is that I wouldn't be where I am today without him."

"Why is that?" asked the young man, curious to know more.

"I met the old man some twenty years ago," explained Mr. Conran. "It was just before Christmas, I was sitting alone at the office party quietly working my way through a bottle of wine and the next thing I knew a little old Chinese man had sat down beside me. I offered him a glass of wine, but he politely refused.

"We started talking and it wasn't long before I was pouring my heart out to him. My life was going nowhere. Despite the fact that I was in my early thirties, I just seemed to be drifting in and out of jobs, and in and out of relationships. It was then that he mentioned the secrets of Abundant Love. I thought it was all a bit of a joke at the time, and the following morning I had only vague recollections of our conversation. In fact, at one point, I thought I must have dreamed the old man up, but when I went through the pockets of the suit I had been wearing, I found a piece of paper containing a list of ten names and telephone numbers."

The young man smiled. It had become a familiar story.

"Needless to say, curiosity got the better of me. I wanted to find out more about the old man and so I contacted the people on the list and it was through them that I learned about the secrets of Abundant Love. Looking back, I can see how those secrets influenced my life. They completely changed my attitude and the way in which I lived my life. I looked at myself and other people in a different light. It was almost as if the world had changed from drab grays to bright colors."

The young man began to take notes as Mr. Conran told his story.

"But the one secret that helped me most at that time in my life," said Mr. Conran, "was . . . the power of commitment. People often assume that love is just about romance and affection, but it is much, much more. Love is about commitment."

"Can you explain?" asked the young man, looking up from his notes.

"Well, it's quite simple really; if you really want to experience love in abundance, if you want to love and be loved, if you really desire lasting loving relationships, you must be committed to being loving. I found out that one of the reasons why I hadn't had a lasting relationship was simply that I was afraid of commitment.

"Why?" asked the young man.

"I can tell you in one word: Fear!"

It was a word the young man had heard several times over the past few weeks. He remembered the old man had said, "Fear is the biggest obstacle to love", and it seemed that most of the secrets of Abundant Love were concerned with overcoming fear, whether it be fear of rejection, fear of ridicule, or fear of loss.

"I think it may have stemmed from my childhood," explained Mr. Conran. "My parents divorced when I was only ten years old and I had seen and felt the pain of separation. I never really knew a stable, secure home or family life. I think that must have played a part in my problem of not being able to commit to anything whether it be to a job, a mortgage or a relationship."

"What I didn't know was that until you can commit yourself to a relationship, you will never be able to create a lasting, loving bond. When you really love someone you are committed to them and to your relationship with them. You make sure that you are always there for them and you put them before anything or anyone else. I believe that if we want anything in life," continued Mr. Conran, "and especially love, we must seek to overcome our fears and be willing to commit to those things and those people who are dear to us.

"Lack of commitment is a common problem, you know. After all, if you have experienced rejection or ridicule or pain in the past you will naturally try to avoid repeating the experience. That is why people who have been hurt in the past subconsciously decide not to allow themselves to get too close to another person. They are not prepared to risk the emotional hurt of separation and loss. Their fear of pain is greater than their desire for love, and so they live in a gray, loveless world, never experiencing the pain of loss but never experiencing the joy of love either. In the end, they deaden their feelings and choose to live their lives in quiet desperation, knowing that there is love to be had, but afraid of the risks and pain when it is lost."

"Well they have a point, don't they?" said the young man.

"Not really. It is like a child saying I don't want any Christmas presents because I might lose them. Personally, I think that the inability of people to commit is one of the main reasons why people have problems with relationships."

"How do you mean?" asked the young man.

"Every relationship has it ups and downs, good times and bad times, yes."

The young man nodded in agreement.

"It is how we deal with those times that is crucial to the survival of a relationship. For instance, if every time a couple had an argument, one or the other threatened to end the relationship, sooner or later the relationship will end because they treat it as expendable. Love is not a priority they are committed to.

"For a relationship to succeed, it must be more important to the two people within it than anything else—more important than their careers or their finances, more important than their cars or their clothes. In short, separation can never be a consideration. It doesn't matter how heated the argument, neither party should ever threaten ending the relationship. Once separation becomes a possibility, however remote, they are heading for trouble.

"If you are committed to something, it doesn't matter what it is, whether it is a job, a relationship, or even a football team, it means that even when things get difficult, quitting is never an option. The problem is that sometimes we simply aren't committed, and so we give up.

"Everyone wants love and loving relationships, but the real question is, 'How committed are you to being loving, and to finding that one special relationship?'"

"What do you mean?" asked the young man, looking up from his notepad.

"Well, let me put it this way; are you committed enough to confront your fears of rejection or failure and do whatever is necessary to create love in your life? Because if you want to experience love and loving relationships in your life, nothing else will do. That is why one of the best questions you can ask yourself when deciding whether a relationship is right for you is simply: 'Am I committed to this person and this relationship?'

"You see, commitment is an essential element of life. After all, a loving mother does not say to her child, 'I'll love you today, but I'm not sure how I will feel tomorrow.' No, she loves her child always, through the good times and through the bad. Problems only begin to occur when we cannot give that commitment. Let me give you an example: I know two men, both of them have a wife and children. One of them spends all of his time at the office or on the golf course, the other deliberately sought out a job which would allow him to spend quality time with his wife and children. Now it doesn't take too much intelligence to guess which man is more likely to create loving relationships."

"So what you are saying," said the young man, "is

that you need to be able to commit yourself to the things that are important to you if you want to have and create love and stability in your life and in the lives of those people you love and who love you."

"I couldn't have put it better myself," smiled Mr. Conran. "What it boils down to is this; love and loving relationships must be more important to you than anything else. Commitment is what distinguishes loving someone from liking someone. I remember seeing a television interview with a U.S. Senator who described his experiences in the second world war when he received severe, crippling injuries to his back. As he related the story, tears began to swell in his eyes. 'My father,' he said, 'travelled by train over three days to come and see me. He was old and his legs were badly crippled with arthritis, yet he stood on that train for three days.' The senator's voice faltered at that point. 'He . . . he must have been in terrible pain, when he arrived his ankles were swollen and blistered . . . but, he made it.'

"Now that's commitment! But no more than millions of parents who make daily sacrifices to do the best they can for their children. They put the needs and desires of their children before their own and before anything else. Commitment is one of the real tests of true love. The simple fact is; if you are not committed to a person, you don't really love them."

"That's an interesting point," said the young man. "Is there no exception to that?"

"None that I can think of. Which brings me back to why I became involved in teaching. As I mentioned, I was drifting through life, uncommitted to anyone or anything. After I met the old man and learned the secrets of Abundant Love, I decided that I wanted to do something worthwhile with my life and share the knowledge that had helped me.

"When I took this job, I had my reservations," confessed Mr. Conrad. "Back then—it must be 20 years ago now—we had terrible problems; some of the children were taking and even selling drugs, there was daily gang fighting both in and outside the school gates, and most of the children were barely able to read when they left school. But that was why I wanted to come here."

"Why would you want to teach in that sort of school?" asked the young man.

"Because it was a challenge. I wanted to make a difference to these children. I read a story about a research project conducted in one of the worst slum areas in Baltimore. A sociology professor at the city university arranged for his undergraduates to visit the schools and write an evaluation of each child's future. Without exception, each report was returned with the words 'Hasn't got a chance' stamped on it. However, 25 years later, another sociology professor decided to follow up the original survey and assigned his students to find out what had happened to those children. Twenty of the children had since moved away and couldn't be traced, but of the remaining 180 children, 176 had achieved extraordinary success, qualifying as lawyers, doctors and respected professionals. So amazed was the professor that he decided to investigate the matter further. Contacting each person in turn, he asked them, 'How do you account for your success?' And in each case, the reply was the same, 'My teacher.'

"Incredibly the teacher was still alive and despite being nearly ninety years of age, she was a robust woman with an alert mind. The professor went to visit her and ask what she did when teaching those children that enabled 176 out of 180 of them—all from a deprived neighborhood—to rise above their circumstances and achieve so much success.

"It's really very simple," said the old lady breaking into a mischievous grin. "I loved those children!"

"When I read that story," said Mr. Conran, "it hit a chord inside me and inspired me to follow that wonderful teacher's example. I knew that with the power of commitment anything could be achieved, so I went back to school and trained to become a teacher, and then I went to work in the schools in the slum neighborhoods. It wasn't easy at first and many times I felt like giving up, but I always remembered that when you're committed, giving up is not an option. And now, as you can see, we have a school to be proud of. These children have at least a chance of succeeding in life, not because they have a special education, but because we care about them, we love them and we are committed to helping them fulfil their true potential."

Later that evening the young man read over the notes he had made of his meeting:

The eighth secret of Abundant Love—the power of commitment.

If you want to have love in abundance, you must be committed to it, and that commitment will be reflected in your thoughts and actions.

Commitment is the true test of love.

If you want to have loving relationships, you must be committed to loving relationships.

When you are committed to someone or something, quitting is never an option.

Commitment distinguishes a fragile relationship from a strong one.

The
POWER
of
PASSION

The following day the young man sat in the office of the ninth person on his list, a man by the name of Peter Serjeant. Mr. Serjeant was a senior executive with a large advertising agency and had a large corner office on the top floor with panoramic views to the south east of the city.

"I first heard about the secrets of Abundant Love over ten years ago," said Mr. Serjeant. "I can remember it as if it were yesterday. I was working late in the office, it was about 8 pm. I had cleared my desk and was thinking about how I was going to tell my wife that I wanted a divorce. I had been thinking about it for weeks. There was a time when we were madly in love, but where and when it all started to go wrong, I don't know. Was there a precise time that we stopped loving each other—a moment, an hour or even a day? Nothing came to mind. All I knew was that we had lost whatever we had, and then stopped trying. There was no love in our marriage any more, we were just going through the motions. Even on the weekends we rarely spent time together. And that night I decided it was time to end the charade. The only solution was to separate.

"The next thing I knew, the office door opened and in walked the cleaner, an old Chinese man whistling Beethoven's fifth symphony."

The young man smiled.

"I asked him what he was so happy about, and he replied, 'You can't help being happy when you're in love.' 'In love?' I said, 'Shouldn't you be past all of that?' 'Love,' he said, 'keeps me feeling young and alive.' 'That must be a great feeling,' I said. 'It is,' he grinned. 'But I'm sure someone like you would know how it feels to be in love.' 'To tell you the truth, it's been a long time,' I answered. 'You sound like someone I know,' he said. 'A friend who is having problems with his marriage. He wants to leave his wife.'

"I felt a lump rise in my throat and my chest tighten as the old man continued. 'They were once deeply in love with each other but over the years they drifted apart. And do you know why?' I shook my head. 'Because they forgot the secrets of Abundant Love!'

"That was the first time I had ever heard of them. He explained that they were ten timeless principles which, when applied, will create love and loving relationships . . . in abundance.

"I was more than a little skeptical at the time. I couldn't believe, whatever these secrets were, that they could help change my relationship with my wife.

As far as I was concerned my marriage had been over for a long time, but I listened to what the old man had to say partly out of politeness and partly out of curiosity, and I had to admit a lot of what he said made sense. Before the old man left, he handed me a piece of paper containing a list of ten names and phone numbers, and he said if I wanted to learn more about the power of the secrets of love, I should contact them.

"I stuffed the note into my pocket and gathered my things to make my way home when the door to the office opened again and in walked another cleaner, this time a woman. I told her that her colleague had already cleaned the room, and then she said something that sent a shiver down my spine—she said she had no colleague with her. She was the only cleaner working in the offices.

"I immediately called the cleaning company who confirmed that there was no such person on their records. It was a complete mystery. The first piece of excitement in my life for some time. In fact I was so intrigued that I had to tell someone about it. I called my wife from the office, something I rarely did. At first she thought something was wrong, but when I told her what had happened, she was almost as excited as I was. I went home and that was the first night in a long time that we sat down together at dinner and really talked. It was almost as if we were beginning an adventure together trying to find out who the old Chinese man was and what the secrets of Abundant Love were all about.

"Over the following weeks my wife and I met the people on the old man's list and we were both literally amazed at the effect the secrets had on our lives. I would never have believed that things so simple could be so important to our lives. All sorts of things began to happen; not only did our relationship improve and the love that we once had return to our marriage, but the relationships with our friends and family and work colleagues also changed. And then one day I woke up and realized what had happened: I was in love again, but not just with my wife—I was in love with life."

"The secrets really had that dramatic an effect?" asked the young man.

"Yes. All of the secrets added a new dimension to my life, but the one secret that had the greatest effect at that time was . . . the power of passion."

"Passion?" exclaimed the young man, looking up from his notepad. "But I thought that love didn't have much to do with sexual attraction."

"It doesn't," said Mr. Serjeant. "Passion is not confined to sex. Passion is a deep interest and enthusiasm. When you are passionate about someone—or something for that matter—you care deeply about them, you have a continual interest in their welfare. That is why if we lose our passion about anything, we lose our feelings of love. After all, if you lose interest or enthusiasm about someone, you are hardly likely to be able to love them."

"No. I suppose not," said the young man.

"Loving relationships need passion," explained Mr. Sergeant. "That is why most relationships start off well. Two people are often passionate about each other when the relationship begins. Both are usually excited, enthusiastic and interested in each other. The problem is, a purely sexual passion just doesn't last. We become bored and disinterested.

"Passion is the magic spark that ignites love and keeps it alive; if you lose that spark, the relationship slowly dies. Not straight away. It takes time. You start out in love and everything is magical, and one day you wake up and the passion has gone and you're no longer in love.

"That was exactly what had happened to my wife and I—all of the passion, the magic and the romance had disappeared."

"But once it's gone, what can you do to bring it back?" asked the young man.

"Create it!" said Mr. Sergeant.

"How can you create passion?" asked the young man. "I thought it is like body chemistry. It is either there or it isn't."

"Passion is simply an overpowering excitement or enthusiasm that focuses our interest," explained Mr. Sergeant. "It can be stimulated by our body chemistry or a strong sexual attraction, but physical passion rarely lasts and cannot be the basis of a lasting, loving relationship. A much stronger passion comes more from our thoughts and our feelings than our body chemistry. When we are interested in something or excited or enthusiastic, we become passionate about it. In a loving relationship this means always focusing on the other person's qualities or characteristics which interest or excite you."

"That sounds all well and good," said the young man, "but sometimes you just get to the point when nothing about a person interests you any more, never mind excites you."

"Then you have to find things in them which do interest you or excite you. Otherwise the relationship will be devoid of passion, and when that happens, it is unlikely that either party is going to be happy in the relationship."

"You know," said the young man thinking aloud, "I think you may be right. Most of my relationships have ended barely after they have begun because I became bored and lost interest in the other person. At first everything is fresh and new and exciting, but as we get to know each other, the relationship becomes stale and boring. But how can you stop it happening? What practical things can you do to keep your passion alive?"

"There are a number of ways to stimulate passion in a relationship," explained Mr. Sergeant. "To begin with, you can recreate passion in a relationship by recreating past experiences when you felt passionate. For example, you could take your partner back to the hotel that you went to on your honeymoon, or book the same restaurant that you went to on your first date.

"You can also introduce spontaneity into your relationship. Surprise your partner occasionally, do things to make her laugh and smile, and a wonderful thing will happen . . . she will invariably reciprocate and do things which will bring a smile to your face. And pretty soon, your relationship is full of surprises. One thing my wife and I did was to make sure that at least once a month we went out together on a date. One month I chose what we did and my wife had to wait to find out what we were going to do until we did it, and the following month, my wife would choose and I had a surprise for the evening. We promised ourselves that whatever happened, we would always have our surprise dates every month.

"When I first learned about the power of passion I consciously did things that I knew my wife would appreciate; I bought her little surprise gifts, I spent more time with her at home and took an interest in her life."

"You mean you didn't take an interest in her life before?" asked the young man.

"Of course I did at first, but then everything became routine. Each day was the same as the last, and I guess over the years the monotony killed any passion that we had for each other. I got so wrapped up in other things like my career that I didn't give much attention to my wife's life. I never really bothered to ask her about her day, about what she did or where she went, but once I started taking an interest in her and her life, something happened . . . she began to take more of an interest in me and my life. And everything snowballed from there."

"We all need things and people to be passionate about if we are to be happy in life. We can be passionate about our work, our beliefs and our leisure pursuits, but most of all we need to be passionate about the people who matter to us. The essence of love and happiness are the same; all we need to do is to live each day with passion."

Later that day the young man read over the notes he had made of his meeting with Mr. Sergeant:

The ninth secret of Abundant Love—the power of passion.

Passion ignites love and keeps it alive.

Lasting passion does not come through physical attraction alone, it comes from deep commitment, enthusiasm, interest and excitement.

Passion can be recreated by recreating past experiences when you felt passionate.

Spontaneity and surprises produce passion.

The essence of love and happiness are the same; all we need to do is to live each day with passion.

The
POWER
of
TRUST

It had been a little over a month since the young man had met the old Chinese man and first heard about the secrets of Abundant Love. There was no doubt that his life had changed for the better . . . but he was still single, no nearer to finding the one special relationship he had always hoped for, and there were still times when he wondered whether he would ever find it. He wanted to believe that there was someone, somewhere waiting for him, but he just couldn't be sure. The final person on the young man's list was Doris Cooper, an elderly woman who lived in a small bungalow in a village situated 20 km to the north of the city. The young man made the journey by car early in the evening and arrived 45 minutes later.

Mrs. Cooper, despite being 87 years of age, still worked as a marriage guidance counsellor. She was a lively woman, bounding with energy and obviously very passionate about her work. In many ways she reminded the young man of the old Chinese gentleman. She had a broad smile and clear aquamarine eyes that sparkled and radiated good health. But there was also something very familiar about her. The young man was certain he had seen her before somewhere, but couldn't quite place her.

Mrs. Cooper greeted the young man with open arms. "Thank you for coming," she said. "I hope the journey was all right."

"It was fine. It took less than an hour door-to-door," the young man assured her.

"Please come in and make yourself at home," said Mrs. Cooper, ushering the young man into the bungalow.

"You seem very familiar," said the young man. "Have we met before?"

"Not to my knowledge," said Mrs. Cooper. "I occasionally write articles for women's magazines."

Mrs. Cooper led the young man into her study which doubled as a private consultation room for her clients. "Would you like a drink?" she asked. "We've got apple or orange juice, a range of teas, you name it."

"Orange juice would be fine, thank you," answered the young man.

Mrs Cooper went for the drinks and left the young man alone. As he looked around the room, the young man was impressed by the number of books Mrs. Cooper had filling two walls of bookshelves, and most were related to psychology, relationships and love. The room was decorated in warm peach and apricot colors, and there was a large oak desk, a sofa and three easy chairs. There were paintings of sunsets and ocean views and on the far wall was a large plaque, the inscription of which the young man couldn't quite make out. He was about to stand up and go over to read it when Mrs. Cooper reentered the room carrying a tray with a jug of orange juice and two glasses.

She sat down on the easy chair next to the young man and handed him a drink.

"I first learned about the secrets of Abundant Love nearly fifty years ago," Mrs. Cooper said as they sat down opposite each other. "I had been married for only two years, but I was very unhappy. I didn't like my husband being away from me for any length of time. As ridiculous as it sounds I got upset if he wanted to spend an evening with his friends or play a round of golf on the weekend. I saw it as him rejecting me. We were always arguing about it; I felt rejected if he chose to do something without me and he said I was suffocating him.

"It all came to a head one weekend during a short holiday we were having by the coast. We hadn't been there for more than ten minutes before my husband was having an intimate conversation with the receptionist, who was a very pretty blonde woman. Naturally, I got extremely upset and we had an almighty row in the hotel reception—I have a terrible temper sometimes. I stormed out and went into the hotel grounds. There was a bench overlooking the sea at the end of the gardens and I sat down there and cried my eyes out. We had come away for the weekend to try and patch up our relationship and within ten minutes we were fighting with each other.

"I don't know how long I had been sitting there when a voice from behind me said, 'Excuse me, are you all right?' I turned around to find an old Chinese man standing beside me.

"I mumbled a response. 'I'm fine thank you.' He looked out to sea and said, 'It's beautiful isn't it?' I looked up and saw the sky turning a deep scarlet on the horizon. It was a beautiful sight but I wasn't in any mood to appreciate the evening sky. I was too upset. And then the old man said, 'In my country we have a saying: Every experience brings with it a lesson which can enrich our lives.' I stayed silent, but he carried on regardless. 'Even when we have problems in our relationships, there is always a lesson, all we have to do is look for it.'

"I looked up at the old man. He must have overheard the argument I had had with my husband. 'Look,' I said, 'I'm sure you have the best intentions but I really . . . ' 'I once had a friend,' he interrupted, 'a beautiful woman, who was married to a fine man. They fell madly in love but a few years later they began arguing—almost every day. And do you know what the root of the problem was? She didn't trust him, and consequently she became possessive and jealous if he was out of her sight or talking to other women. As a consequence he began to feel suffocated and trapped. Her fears were driving away the man she loved.'

"I turned to face the old man. 'Why did she do it?' I asked. 'She probably had good cause.' 'Actually no. Her husband had done nothing wrong. She was just a very insecure woman. It was understandable too; her father was a philanderer and after a number of affairs, left her mother. The most important man in her life had left her and her mother and consequently, subconsciously she didn't trust men.'

"I felt a lump swell in my chest. It was as if that old man was reciting my life. 'Do you know it is a funny thing,' he said, 'but the difficulties we have in our relationships are often a result of the problems we have carried from our childhood.' 'You may be right,' I said. 'We are all controlled by our childhood experiences.' 'Only if we allow ourselves to be controlled by our past,' he said. 'This was an important lesson she learned from her problems with her marriage. The past does not have to equal the future. Whatever our past, whatever our experiences, we all have the power to change.'

"I asked him if the woman had managed to change. Did her marriage survive? And he told me that not only did the woman's marriage survive but that they loved each other more now than the day they were married. 'How did she do it?' I asked. 'The secrets of Abundant Love,' he said. I hadn't a clue what he was talking about but he then handed me a piece of paper. I looked at it briefly and saw that it contained a list of ten names and telephone numbers and when I looked back up, he was gone.

"I went back to the hotel reception to find out which room the old Chinese man was staying in. The woman my husband had been talking to earlier was still at the desk. I apologized for my earlier outburst and then she told me that all my husband had asked her was if she could recommend some restaurants in the area. He wanted to surprise me and take me out for a special dinner! The old man had been right. It was my insecurities that were causing my problems.

"I asked if she could tell me which room the old Chinese man was staying in and then she told me that there was no Chinese man staying at the hotel. There were no Chinese employees either!

"I went to our room and found my husband. He was still pretty upset. I apologized for reacting the way I did and told him how ashamed I was when I found out that he had only been talking to the receptionist to find a restaurant to take me to for dinner. I told him about my meeting with the old Chinese man and the secrets of Abundant Love. He said that something would have to change because we couldn't go on the way we had been for the past two years, always fighting and arguing.

"So the following week I called the people on the old man's list to find out about the secrets and to see if what the old man said was really possible."

"What?" asked the young man.

"That we all have the power to change."

"And is it?" asked the young man.

"Definitely. All of the secrets of Abundant Love are important because they all help us to create love and build loving relationships, but the one that made the biggest difference in my life was . . . the power of trust."

"Trust?" said the young man. "What has that got to do with love?"

"If we don't trust someone, we can't love them."

"Why not?" asked the young man.

"Because without trust, we become suspicious, anxious and to some extent frightened that the person will betray us. That can put unbearable pressure on a relationship—one partner feels anxious, the other feels trapped.

"One thing you have to remember is that when you know and apply the secrets of Abundant Love in your life, the chances of your marriage being successful are multiplied because you're aware of the things which are necessary to nurture loving relationships. You would only get married or settle down with someone if you were one hundred percent committed to the relationship. Your partner is unlikely to feel threatened, unloved or distrustful if you are communicating with her, and letting her know that you love her."

"So you're saying that if you can't trust someone, the relationship is doomed?" asked the young man.

"Absolutely. That is why one of the best questions you can ask yourself if you are unsure about settling down with someone is: 'Do I trust them completely and unreservedly?' If the answer is 'no' you would probably want to think carefully about the relationship before committing yourself to it. And it works both ways of course, the other person also needs to have complete trust in you.

"One of the most important lessons I ever learned was that trust is an essential ingredient in all loving relationships. Not only do you need to be able to trust in the other person, but you also have to be able to trust in the relationship itself."

"What do you mean by that?" asked the young man.

"Well, some people worry about the possibility of a relationship ending. They think to themselves, 'This is too good to be true. It can't last.' I mean, these days many people get nervous about getting married simply because of the high divorce rate. They worry about the relationship ending before it has even started."

The young man felt his face flush. They were his words almost verbatim when he had met the old Chinese man weeks earlier. He cleared his throat. "Yes, but they do have a point though, don't they?"

"In what way?" replied Mrs. Cooper.

"Well, there is a high rate of divorce and so the odds of a marriage being successful are not particularly good."

"Yes, but the odds of a marriage being successful are still higher than the odds that it will end in divorce. Focusing on the possibility of divorce only makes it more likely. That is why it is important to trust in your relationship; to act as if, come hell or high water, the relationship will never end."

"How does that help?" asked the young man.

"Remember that thoughts and fears can be self-fulfilling. If you imagine problems, your fears will be reflected in your behavior and you will often then create problems. This is exactly what happened to me. Because I didn't trust my husband, I became obsessively jealous and nearly drove him away."

"I see what you mean," said the young man.

"Many people create problems in their lives before they exist. But such an attitude is not conducive to love and happiness. The only way round it is to learn to trust—yourself, your partner and life. And, on the other side of the coin, it is equally important to behave in a trustworthy way so that your partner has no real cause to feel insecure."

"But how can you learn how to trust people if your problems go back to your childhood?" asked the young man. "Surely you would need years of therapy?"

"Not necessarily. Come with me," Mrs. Cooper said, gesturing for him to follow her to the other side of the room. She pointed to the plaque that the young man noticed earlier. It read:

"Life changes when we change."

"This inscription is one of the most powerful quotes I ever came across because it says that we don't have to be victims of the past. We all have the power to change. As the old man said to me, 'the past does not have to equal the future.' We write the book of Life. The next page doesn't have to be the same as the last. We can begin a new chapter, and this is what the secrets of Abundant Love enable us to do—change! It doesn't matter what has happened in the past; whether you are having problems with relationships or finding it difficult to attract loving relationships, with the secrets of Abundant Love, you can change.

"I have met so many people who get totally despondent about being single and think that they will never find a lasting, loving relationship. I have also known lots of people who feel trapped in a loveless, unhappy relationship. Sometimes they give up hope, they become disillusioned, bitter and cynical. They think they are victims and so they become victims and go through life feeling isolated and alone, or trapped, hoping that one day someone special will enter their lives and change everything for them. But the truth is that the only person who has the power to change anything in your life is you. Nobody else."

Just then the front door opened and in walked an old man dressed in a large overcoat. Mrs. Cooper introduced her husband to the young man. As he took off his coat the young man suddenly realized where he had seen Mrs. Cooper and her husband before.

"Now I remember," he said, clicking his fingers. "Were you both at a wedding about a month ago? Mark Elkin and Sonia Spaid."

Mr. Cooper raised an eyebrow, "Yes, we were there. Why do you ask?"

"That's where I saw you. I noticed you both dancing together. I remember thinking how much in love you both looked and wondering what your secret was."

"Well, now you know," said Mrs. Cooper smiling.

"So you saw the old Chinese man at the wedding as well," said the young man.

"The old Chinese man was at Mark and Sonia's wedding?" exclaimed Mrs. Cooper.

"That was where I met him," said the young man.

Later that night the young man read over his notes:

The tenth secret of Abundant Love—the power of trust.

Trust is essential in all loving relationships. Without it one person becomes suspicious, anxious and fearful and the other person feels trapped and emotionally suffocated.

You cannot love someone completely unless you trust them completely.

Act as if your relationship with the person you love will never end.

One of the ways you can tell whether a person is right for you is to ask yourself, "Do I trust them completely and unreservedly?" If the answer is "no", think carefully before making a commitment.

EPILOGUE

The young man sat by himself surveying the scene. It had not been as grand or extravagant as some of the other weddings he had been to, but there was a lively, friendly atmosphere, and the hundred or so guests were clearly enjoying themselves. As the band started to warm up, the young man's mind drifted back two years to the wedding at which he had met the old Chinese man. He couldn't help smiling to himself as he remembered how cynical about love he had been back then.

He smiled as he remembered visiting the people on the old man's list. Although they had all sounded sincere and inspiring, at the back of his mind there had been an area of doubt. He had been unsure whether the secrets of Abundant Love would work for him. But there was no doubt that they had worked for others—people who, like him, had been searching for love and loving relationships, people who had become disillusioned with life and led a cold, lonely existence, and even people who found themselves in unhappy, troubled relationships.

The young man had written out three lists in a small notebook which summarized the secrets of Abundant Love and how they could be applied to different situations in life, and he carried the notebook wherever he went so that he could always refer to them for inspiration in difficult times and pass on the secrets to others.

The summaries read:

The ten secrets of Abundant Love—creating love in your life.

1. Choose loving thoughts.
2. Learn to respect yourself and others.
3. Focus on what you can give rather than on what you can take.
4. To find love, first find a friend.
5. Hug people. Open your arms and you open your heart.
6. Let go of fears, prejudices and judgments.
7. Communicate your feelings.
8. Be committed—make love your number one priority.
9. Live with passion.
10. Trust others, trust yourself and trust life.

The ten secrets of Abundant Love—how to recognize your life partner.

1. Does he/she have the physical, emotional, intellectual and spiritual qualities that you need from a life partner?
2. Do you respect him/her?
3. What will you be able to give him/her to fulfil his/her needs?
4. Is he/she your best friend? Do you have common goals and ambitions, common values and common beliefs?
5. When you hold each other, does it feel like you belong?
6. Do you give each other space and freedom to grow and to learn?
7. Can you communicate honestly and openly with each other?
8. Are you both committed to the relationship?
9. Do you feel strongly and passionately about him/her and your relationship? Does he/she mean more to you than anything else?
10. Do you trust each other completely?

The ten secrets of Abundant Love—how to bring love back into your relationship.

1. Think about your partner's needs and desires as well as your own.
2. Learn to respect yourself and your partner. Ask "What do I respect about myself?" and "What do I respect about my partner?"

3. Focus on what you might not be giving to the relationship rather than on what you think you should be taking.
4. Make friends with your partner. Seek common interests, common pursuits.
5. Hug, touch affectionately, and open your arms to your partner.
6. Let go of the past and forgive. Make a new start.
7. Communicate your feelings openly and honestly.
8. Commit yourself to the relationship. Put your partner at the top of your list of priorities.
9. Recreate passion in your relationship.
10. Learn to trust your partner, trust your relationship and act as if it will never end.

As he slowly incorporated the ten secrets of Abundant Love into his own life, he began to notice changes. Nothing obvious, nothing tangible. There was no particular change in his outward appearance, nothing you could put your finger on at any rate, but nevertheless, important changes, profound changes had taken place.

His family and friends and even his work colleagues noticed his behavior had altered. He greeted them with open arms and a hug instead of a formal handshake. And he spoke to people differently; attentively, respectfully, always looking them in the eye. He always made time for people and showed a genuine interest and concern for them. He made a point to remember other people's birthdays, or call someone he hadn't seen for some time, just to say "hello" and let them know he was thinking about them. But what was most strange was that he would often do spontaneous acts of kindness. It was not uncommon for him to buy a bunch of flowers and, without saying a word, hand it to a stranger on the street just to see the expression of bewilderment and amusement in their faces. He got pleasure just from seeing someone smile.

And his close friends noticed that he was no longer preoccupied with finding someone to love. Unbeknown to them, the young man concentrated on being loving, trusting that his love would return to him and that at the right time and in the right place, he would meet the girl of his dreams.

Some of his colleagues and friends asked him what brought about this change in him. Was it a new found religious belief, or had he come into money? Or was he on something, a mood enhancing drug? Few believed him when he told them the story of his meeting with a little old Chinese man and the secrets of Abundant Love. But there were those who listened to his story with an open mind and invariably, months later, they would call him to thank him and tell him what a difference the secrets had made to their lives.

Then, quite out of the blue, something wonderful happened. He was at home one evening when he received a phone call. It was a young woman who asked if she could meet with him. She explained she had been given his phone number by an old Chinese man. "Something about secrets of Abundant Love," she said. He met her the following day and was instantly attracted to her, not just by the warmth of her eyes or the beauty in her face. As they talked he felt as if he had finally met a kindred spirit, someone he could talk freely to about things that mattered to him.

And now she was walking toward him with an outstretched hand, her physical beauty matched only by the gentleness and beauty of her soul. Everything seemed to happen in slow motion. Looking at her, he was momentarily breathless, overwhelmed with feelings of love. It was a moment he would remember for the rest of his life, the first moment when he understood what it meant to have love in abundance.

It was the moment he had always dreamed of but, until his meeting with the old man, had never really believed would be his. What the young man would have done to get in contact with the old man just to thank him, to let him at least know how he had helped change his life. How he wished he could have invited him to his wedding.

Everyone in the room stood up cheering and applauding as the young man took her hand and led her toward the dance floor. He was dressed immaculately in a light gray, double-breasted suit but, as he held her hand, all eyes were on the woman at his side. She was wearing a simple but elegant off-the-shoulder white satin dress which complimented her natural beauty.

As they reached the center of the dance floor, they turned toward each other and gazed into each other's eyes. The cheers and wolf whistles died down and the band began to play their song; *The Power of Love*. The young man looked up at the smiling faces of his family and friends clapping and cheering. But as he looked around the room his attention was caught by a lone figure standing at the back of the hall by the exit. It was him! The old Chinese man was standing alone, smiling.

Adam J. Jackson is an internationally renowned therapist, author, and motivational speaker. He originally practiced law in England before retraining in natural health sciences. He currently lives in the United Kingdom and heads health clinics both there and in Toronto, Canada.

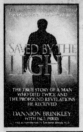